The American Harvest Cookbook

The American Harvest Cookbook

Cooking with squash, zucchini, pumpkins, and more

Rosemary Moon

CHARTWELL
BOOKS, INC.

A QUINTET BOOK

Published by Chartwell Books
A Division of Book Sales, Inc.
114, Northfield Avenue
Edison, New Jersey 08837

This edition produced for sale in the U.S.A.,
its territories and dependencies only.

ISBN 0-7858-0898-1

This book was designed and produced by
Quintet Publishing Limited
6 Blundell Street
London N7 9BH

Creative Director: Richard Dewing
Art Director: Silke Braun
Designer: Rita Wüthrich
Senior Editor: Sally Green
Editor: Rosie Hankin
Photographer: Ferguson Hill
Food Stylist: Kathryn Hawkins

Typeset in Great Britain by
Central Southern Typesetters, Eastbourne
Manufactured in Singapore by Pica Colour Separation Overseas Pte Ltd.
Printed in Singapore by Star Standard Industries Pte Ltd.

Contents

Introduction

Cucumbers, melons, pumpkins, and squashes are all part of the same family as gourds, and it is highly likely that hard-skinned, prickly gourds were used as weapons long before anyone thought of eating them or their relatives. What is certain is that they were growing between three and five thousand years ago in Peru, but it is assumed that they were originally native to Africa. The most popular theory for their arrival in South America is that they were carried by Polynesian voyagers crossing the great oceans. Many centuries later, they were "discovered" by Columbus and the Spanish, and taken to Europe.

Gourds have featured in the ancient history of peoples around the world. In India they were used as water carriers, and they are mentioned in Chinese history some 400 years before Confucius. It is therefore thought by some that, because the seeds of the whole family are so durable, they may well have been washed from one continent to another by the sea. Whatever the truth of the matter, it is indisputable that gourds, pumpkins, and squashes are popular and valuable crops throughout the world.

Although pumpkins, squashes, cucumbers, and melons are all related, they are a diverse range of fruits. The distinction between them is more based on area of origin: pumpkins and squashes are native to the New World of the Americas, and the word "squash" is from the American Indian word *askutasquash*; melons and cucumbers, however, were known of in or before Old Testament times in the Old World, and are generally grouped into the family of gourds, a word coming from the Latin *cucurbita*. So, you might argue that an American harvest would comprise only pumpkins and squashes, based on origins, but as cucumbers, large zucchini, and melons are enjoyed throughout the world, I have kept the family together within the pages of this book, although pumpkins and squashes are definitely the main ingredients.

Gourds are usually much smaller than pumpkins and squashes and may be edible or decorative. They are often fascinating in shape—

Above *Everyone is familiar with the large orange pumpkins used as lanterns at Halloween.*

Right *A fine display of pumpkins and squashes, including many varieties from around the world.*

Pumpkins and squashes are both edible and decorative.

crook necked, penguin, or bottle shaped, smooth-skinned, warty, and possibly multicolored. Throughout history they have been put to decorative or practical uses—water carriers, storage pots, vases, musical instruments, rattles, and lamp bases. The chayote is one of the best-known edible gourds, and was originally grown in South and Central America, but is now popular in China as well, where it is sliced and stir-fried. I have not included edible gourds in this book as there was so much to say about the commoner edible fruits.

For many years the perception of pumpkins has been of a rather bland ingredient, watery, and without much flavour—something to make into a pie at Thanksgiving but that is largely ignored for the rest of the year. But the members of this fruit family are extremely versatile—they are good in savory dishes, and also excellent in pies and ice creams too. As I have explored the varieties of pumpkins and squashes for my recipes, and experimented on friends and family, we have all reached the same conclusion: they are deliciously versatile and we should all be far more adventurous with them. I hope my recipes will inspire you in your kitchen.

Pumpkin Varieties

I really don't think that as cooks we need to get side-tracked into the business of classifying the foods we eat into their correct scientific or botanical families. However, some basic knowledge of the varieties can be quite useful. For example, the big orange pumpkin that we all think of for lanterns and soup is *Cucurbita pepo*, as are the spaghetti marrow or squash, zucchini, and other soft-skinned varieties. These are summer squashes and do not store well. Winter varieties, such as acorn, butternut, crown prince, and Hubbard all have harder skins and do store—through the winter—and are *Cucurbita maxima* or *Cucurbita moschata*. Most winter squashes can be substituted one for another in recipes, although you will quickly find which is your favorite and go back to that time and again.

Growing Pumpkins

All melons, cucumbers, pumpkins, and large zucchini grow on sprawling, vine-like plants, although modern bush varieties take up slightly less room, or may be trained upward to economize on space in the garden. Pumpkins and large zucchini are generally easy to cultivate but they do take up a vast amount of room, especially if it is your dream to grow the award-winning, biggest pumpkin of all time. They like lots of sun and nutrient-rich soil, which is why they are often found trailing over the compost heap. They also need a lot of water. To ensure the maximum time for the fruits to develop, it is best to sow the seeds under glass and bring the plants on at the beginning of the season, before hardening them off after the last frost and then planting them out. No members of this family like frost at the beginning or end of their lives.

If you buy a squash or pumpkin that you particularly like, it is always worth saving a few seeds from it to grow on the next year. In order to get large fruits I always restrict my pumpkins to about four fruits a plant, pinching out or stopping the shoots after the fruits have set, so that all the goodness and effort is concentrated on the tasks of growing and ripening. If you intend to store squashes for later use, they should be left in the sun for 10 to 14 days after cutting, to allow the skins to harden. This will encourage them to keep well in a frost-free, ventilated shed.

Cucumbers and melons are also grown on vines, but they tend to be trained in an upright habit in greenhouses to achieve the necessary temperatures. Melons need to be supported as they ripen—the fruits can get very heavy—and keen gardeners will have net hammocks or slings for them. (A pair of pantihose may serve as a substitute.)

Like all the gourds, cucumbers grow on vine-like plants, and appreciate very rich soil and a lot of sun and water.

Cucumbers are either smooth-skinned and long (these varieties must be grown under glass) or smaller and ridged. The latter, which I find to be slightly more bitter in flavor, may be grown outside.

Cucumbers may be straight or curved. There are some unusual varieties, including tiny, prickly round ones, sometimes called hairy spiky cucumbers, although also known as squirting cucumbers, because of their method of ejecting their seeds for distribution. The massive Armenian cucumbers which have a speckled green and cream flesh are known, accurately, as Armenian yard-longs, whereas regular Armenian varieties only grow to 16 to 18 inches. Lebanese cucumbers are a similar shape, dark green in color but grow only about eight or nine inches long. And the baby of them all, the Jamaican, is apple green in color, egg shaped, and only about one and a half inches long.

Melons need to be supported as they ripen as the fruits become very heavy.

Ripeness in Melons

The most useful tip that I can offer with regard to selecting a ripe and juicy melon is that they will be fragrant when ready to eat. Only press a melon gently at the end—it should give a little—otherwise the flesh will bruise, but do sniff before buying at the supermarket. This works well for most varieties except honeydews, which have a harder, more impermeable skin. Ripe melons should be seductively fragrant.

Probably the only way to be certain of the sweetness and juiciness of a watermelon before cutting into it is by looking at the stem. When the flesh is ready to eat it should be slightly sunken into the top of the melon, and roughened with bumps and calluses. Of course, if it has been trimmed ready for sale this is no guide at all.

Pumpkins and squashes are native to the warmer parts of the Americas, but they are now grown successfully in many parts of the world, and are a popular, as well as economically important, crop.

United States

Without doubt the most common variety in the United States is the big, orange pumpkin. That's a bit of a loose description, as there are actually lots of different varieties that are all very similar. Because they are watery in comparison to the firmer squashes, I prefer not to boil them as they can very easily cook to a mush. Dice and steam them if you will, or cook in olive oil or butter with freshly grated nutmeg or black pepper. They are also good in soups, especially when combined with a stronger-flavored vegetable, such as carrot or swede. The cooked flesh may also be puréed and used in numerous sweet or savory dishes.

Orange pumpkins—America's most popular variety.

Of all the squashes the butternut is one of the most popular. It is native to tropical America, but is now widely cultivated in the north. It is naturally pear-shaped, although it may remain cylindrical if growing conditions are not quite warm enough. The flesh is dramatically orange, and it bakes, roasts, and stews well. It is one of my favorite varieties for soups, especially with orange. The banana squash is very good for curries as it is dry and firm-fleshed, and retains its shape when cooked. Another American variety, the golden nugget, is usually eaten when young with a soft skin. The flesh has a green tinge and it may be stuffed and baked like a large zucchini.

The acorn squash can be green or yellow, or both.

Canada

The most famous of the Canadian squashes is the acorn, although this is now also very popular next door in the United States. Acorns are usually green-skinned, but they do turn yellow. They are hard-skinned and ridged, which makes them very difficult to peel before cooking. I usually cut them in half to bake, or cut them into rings to fry. The skin can be cut off easily once the flesh is cooked. Blue Hubbards, which have very hard, warty skins, grow to be very large indeed and can be very difficult to cut into although, strangely enough, rabbits seem to have no difficulty in munching their way into them. This Canadian variety is also widely grown elsewhere.

Australia and New Zealand

The most famous of the Australian varieties is the Queensland blue which, like the blue Hubbard, can grow to an enormous size. It has a very good flavor and texture, and becomes really creamy when mashed with butter after boiling or steaming. The snake squash is native to Australia and Southeast Asia, and is pale green in color. Because it grows like a curled snake it is best eaten young, when the skin is tender, so that it can be sliced into distinctive rounds before cooking. The flavor is greatly enhanced by herbs.

Some of my favorite squashes are native to New Zealand, where they are promoted as an excellent vegetable for the modern health-conscious diet. My number one favorite is the crown prince, a

Right Despite its gray skin, the crown prince squash has a vibrant orange flesh.

Kabocha squashes

Onion squash

Gem squash

smooth, hard-skinned variety with a gray skin and vibrant orange flesh. It pan-fries and stir-fries well, it bakes and roasts, and it makes full-flavored, smooth soups. Crown prince is also very tasty cold, making it an excellent choice for salads.

Other New Zealand varieties include the buttercup (also popular in the United States) and the kabocha. The latter is usually green-skinned and, like the crown prince, has bright orange flesh. It bakes and fries well, and I often use it in breads. The red kabocha is less well known but some consider it to have a finer and more distinctive flavor than the standard variety.

Japan

Popular in New Zealand, but also a firm favorite in Japan, the uchiki kuri is more popularly known as the onion squash, especially in the West. It is easy to see how this name evolved, as the deep orange skin has very distinct onion markings. The squash is best baked after scooping out the seeds. I sometimes start it off in a hot oven, and then add a filling. Cover with foil, at least for part of the cooking time, to prevent the flesh from drying out before it is tender. Another popular Japanese squash is the kumikuri, an orange and green variety with orange ribs.

South Africa

Squashes are very popular in South Africa, and some of the best known are the butternut, the golden Hubbard, and the tiny round gem squash. Gems are best pierced two or three times with a fork and then boiled—scoop the seeds out once the squash is cooked. They can also be peeled and sliced, and then fried.

The rolet, which is very similar to the gem, is actually native to Zimbabwe and is cooked in the same way. The skin is a slightly deeper green, but, apart from that I can detect very little difference between the two.

France

Pumpkins are very popular in France. The French prefer ridged, deep orange pumpkins to the paler varieties, and they also grow many Turk's caps, an orange squash with a striped green and white center which gives this distinctive variety its name. Although it is delicious to eat and may be stuffed, once well colored and ripened, the skin will harden and become very difficult to cut. Many people end up using these colorful squashes simply for decorative purposes.

Cooking the Squash Recipes

Many of my recipes start by roasting pumpkin or squash before going on to use it in other ways. I have a big range cooker at home which is always on, so I simply roast slices of squash in the constantly hot oven before I purée or chop the flesh. However, to put a regular oven on just for this would be rather extravagant. If you are using the oven and there is a little room to spare, even if the oven is set at a lower temperature, do take the opportunity to roast or bake some pumpkin or squash slices for later use. Just cook them until they are tender. They keep well when wrapped up in the fridge—indeed they keep better that way than leaving a cut pumpkin out in the kitchen.

Sliced or diced pumpkin and squash may also be steamed if you prefer, or cooked in the microwave. Microwave cookbooks will suggest a suitable timing, but it would generally be about 5 minutes on High per pound depending on the oven. Microwave cooking is more suitable for preparing the flesh for purées than for salads—diced squash or pumpkin could be pan-fried for the latter use, although this may increase the fat content of the finished dish.

Cutting Pumpkins and Squashes

One reason why I roast the pumpkin or squash for so many of my recipes is that it makes actually peeling the skin away so much easier. Some of the winter squash varieties, especially those with very hard skins, can be very difficult to cut into and to peel. I find that the best knife to use is a butcher's knife, with a slightly rounded end to the blade. This seems to give slightly better leverage than the more traditional cook's knife. A cleaver would undoubtedly make the task of the initial cut somewhat easier—but do take care! Persevere—the following recipes prove that the effort expended in preparation really is worthwhile.

Pumpkin Seeds— a Delicious Nibble

I have never actually toasted squash seeds—they seem rather hard—but pumpkin seeds do make an excellent nibble, a good alternative to peanuts.

Scrape them out of the pumpkin and pull off any stringy flesh, then wash them well and leave them to dry on paper towels.

Once dry, the seeds can be grilled, or dry-fried in a nonstick frying pan.

Season them while still hot— I usually just add milled sea salt—then toss them from time to time in the seasoning until completely cold.

Munch immediately, or store in a screw-top jar.

Chilled Cucumber and Green Chile Soup

Roasted Acorn Soup with Cucumber Salsa

Mediterranean Roasted Pumpkin Soup

Butternut and Orange Soup

Pumpkin, Lentil, and Bacon Soup

Melon and Pesto Soup

Pumpkin, Carrot, and Lovage Soup

Baked Gem Squash with Parmesan Cream

Baked Limed Zucchini in Cream

Melon with Figs and Prosciutto

Pumpkin, Bacon, and Tomato Skewers

Roast Crown Prince Squash and Pistachio Pâté

Curried Lamb and Pumpkin Koftas

Spiced Minted Melon Balls

Pumpkin Chutney

Butternut and Chicken Liver Pâté

Pumpkin Relish

Cucumber and Radish Raita

Soups, Appetizers, & Relishes

Chilled Cucumber and Green Chile Soup

This soup is highly spiced which counteracts the "flavor numbing" effect of chilling. Traditional Thai seasonings make it very refreshing.

SERVES 6

- 4 large scallions, trimmed and sliced
- 1 stalk lemon grass, bruised and chopped fine
- 1–2 garlic cloves, crushed
- 2 each green and caribe chiles, deseeded and chopped fine, or 3 green chiles
- 2 lime leaves, shredded fine
- 1 vegetable stock cube, crumbled
- 4 cups water
- 1 large cucumber, weighing about 1 lb, deseeded and chopped
- 1 cup unsweetened yogurt
- 1 Tbsp fish sauce
- Salt, to taste
- 2 Tbsp chopped fresh cilantro leaves

Preparation: 1 hour 10 minutes
Chilling time: 2–3 hours

❶ Place the scallions, lemon grass, garlic, chiles, and lime leaves in a large saucepan with the crumbled stock cube. Pour in the water, then bring to a boil. Add the cucumber, then cover the pan completely and remove from the heat, and leave to marinate for 1 hour.

❷ Purée the soup in a blender or food processor until smooth, then press the mixture through a fine sieve with the back of a ladle. Whisk in the yogurt and fish sauce, then season the soup to taste with a little salt if necessary. Chill very well, for at least 2 hours.

❸ Add the cilantro to the soup just before serving, and spoon the soup over about a tablespoon of crushed ice in each individual bowl.

TIP

Fresh herbs have been used throughout this book. However, dried herbs could always be substituted. Use 1 tsp dried for every Tbsp fresh herbs.

Roasted Acorn Soup with Cucumber Salsa

This creamy, nutty flavored soup is further enhanced by a subtly spicy cucumber salsa.

SERVES 4

- 1 acorn squash (weighing about 1 lb 4 oz) quartered
- Salt and freshly grated nutmeg
- Olive oil
- 1 large onion, chopped fine
- 2 slices bacon, rinded and chopped
- 2 large carrots, sliced
- 4–5 arugula, shredded fine, or 3 bay leaves
- 4 cups well-flavored vegetable stock
- Ground black pepper
- 1 cup milk

FOR THE SALSA

- 1 Tbsp coriander seeds
- ½ medium cucumber, deseeded and diced
- 1 mild green chile, deseeded and chopped very fine
- 1 small red onion, chopped fine
- 1 fresh tomato, deseeded and chopped
- 1 garlic clove, chopped fine
- 1-in piece fresh ginger root, shredded

Preparation: 50 minutes
Cooking time: 45 minutes

❶ Preheat a 425°F oven. Scrape the seeds out of the squash, then arrange the pieces in a roasting pan, and season lightly with salt and nutmeg. Drizzle with a little olive oil, then roast the squash for 45 minutes, or until tender. Then leave to cool.

❷ Meanwhile, cook the onion, bacon, and carrots with 1 tablespoon of olive oil in a covered pan for 4 to 5 minutes, until the vegetables are tender. Scoop the roasted squash from the skin, chop it roughly, then add it to the pan with the lovage or bay, and stock. Season lightly with salt and pepper, then bring to a boil. Cover the pan and simmer for 30 minutes.

❸ Meanwhile, prepare the salsa. Heat a small frying pan over medium heat until hot, then add the coriander seeds and fry for about 1 minute, until roasted and fragrant. Crush the seeds lightly using a pestle and mortar, or use the end of a rolling pin. Add all the other salsa ingredients except the ginger. Finally, gather up the ginger shreds in your hands and squeeze just the juice into the mixture. Leave to stand for about 30 minutes, to allow the flavors to blend.

❹ Cool the soup slightly, then blend until smooth in a blender or food processor, adding the milk. Season to taste and reheat if necessary. Serve the soup with a generous spoonful of salsa in each portion.

TIP

Roasting hard-skinned squashes before their final cooking has two advantages: it makes them easier to cut and prepare and it brings out their naturally nutty flavor.

soups, appetizers, & relishes

Mediterranean Roasted Pumpkin Soup

A really raunchy soup to serve before an equally powerful main course! Blend the olives into the soup if you prefer.

SERVES 4

- 6 x 1-in slices pumpkin, deseeded (about 1 lb 10 oz in total)
- 6 large tomatoes, halved
- 1 large onion, sliced thick
- 4–5 garlic cloves
- 4 sprigs fresh rosemary
- Salt and ground black pepper
- Olive oil
- 2 cups water or stock
- ½ cup pitted black olives, chopped
- Shavings of fresh Parmesan cheese
- Olive oil bread, to serve

Preparation: 10 minutes

Cooking time: 1 hour

❶ Preheat a 425°F oven. Arrange the vegetables in a large roasting pan and tuck in the rosemary. Season well, then drizzle with olive oil. Roast for 40 to 50 minutes, until starting to blacken. Allow the vegetables to cool.

❷ Cut the flesh away from the skin of the pumpkin and chop roughly.

Remove the rosemary, then scrape all the vegetables into a blender or food processor, and add the pumpkin flesh. Blend until smooth, then rub the soup through a fine sieve into a saucepan.

❸ Add the water or stock, then heat the soup slowly until almost at a boil. Season, then stir in the chopped olives. Ladle into warmed bowls, and garnish with a few shavings of Parmesan.

Butternut and Orange Soup

This was one of the first squash dishes that I ever tasted and has remained a firm favorite ever since!

SERVES 4–6

- 1 onion, chopped
- 2 Tbsp olive oil
- 1–2 butternut squashes (about 2 lb in total), peeled and diced
- Grated zest and juice of 2 oranges
- 3 pt well-flavored vegetable stock
- Salt and ground black pepper
- 2 bay leaves
- Freshly grated nutmeg
- 2 Tbsp chopped fresh parsley

Preparation: 10 minutes

Cooking time: 45 minutes

❶ Cook the onion in the oil until softened, then add the squash, and cook slowly for 5 minutes, stirring occasionally. Stir in the grated orange, then add the stock, seasoning, bay leaves, and nutmeg. Bring the soup to a boil, then cover, and simmer for 40 minutes, until the squash is tender.

❷ Allow the soup to cool slightly, remove the bay leaves, then blend in a blender or food processor until smooth. Rinse the pan and return the soup to it, adding the orange juice. Reheat the soup slowly—do not let it boil—then season to taste, and add the freshly chopped parsley just before serving.

20

Mediterranean Roasted Pumpkin Soup

Pumpkin, Lentil, and Bacon Soup

Lentils and bacon add a smoky flavor to this creamy pumpkin soup.

SERVES 4–6
- 1 onion, chopped fine
- 4 slices smoked back bacon, rinded and chopped
- 2 Tbsp olive oil
- 2 garlic cloves, sliced fine
- 3 cups peeled, seeded, and diced pumpkin
- ½ cup red lentils
- 14-oz can chopped tomatoes
- 4 sprigs fresh thyme
- 2 bay leaves
- Salt and ground black pepper
- 4 cups well-flavored vegetable stock
- ⅔ cup whipping cream

Preparation: 15 minutes
Cooking time: 40 minutes

❶ Cook the onion and bacon in the oil for 5 minutes over low heat, until the onions are soft but not browned. Add the garlic and the pumpkin, and cook for 2 minutes more, then stir in the lentils.

❷ Add the seasonings, then pour in the stock. Bring the soup to a boil, then simmer slowly for 30 to 40 minutes, until the pumpkin and lentils are tender.

❸ Allow the soup to cool slightly, then remove the thyme and bay leaves, before blending in a blender or food processor until smooth. Add extra salt and pepper to taste, then ladle the soup into warmed bowls. Add a swirl of cream to each helping before serving.

Melon and Pesto Soup

A chilled melon soup that is perfect for summer entertaining as it actually benefits from being made up to a day in advance. The pesto redeems the flavor of the fruit beautifully. It's also a marvelous way of using up the shells of melons that you have balled for other dishes.

SERVES 4
- 4 cups Galia melon purée (made from 2 melons)
- 1 mild green chile, deseeded and chopped very fine
- ⅔ cup water
- 3 Tbsp best quality pesto sauce
- Salt and white pepper
- Lime juice, to taste

Preparation: 15 minutes
Chilling time: 2 hours

❶ Blend the melon purée with all the remaining ingredients, adding just enough lime juice to lift the flavor of the soup.

❷ Chill the soup for at least 2 hours, then serve over a little crushed ice. Crisp toasts made with Italian bread and flavored with a mild garlic butter are a perfect accompaniment.

TIP

It is essential to use the very best pesto sauce—it should be slightly sweet, and made just with basil, garlic, Parmesan, pine nuts, and olive oil.

Melon and Pesto Soup

Pumpkin, Carrot, and Lovage Soup

I like to add carrots to this soup, to give a little more texture and flavor as I use the main crop orange pumpkin. This is an excellent recipe for using up the inside of a Halloween pumpkin.

SERVES 6

- 1 large onion, chopped
- 3 Tbsp olive oil
- 3 cups peeled, seeded, and diced pumpkin
- 1½ cups diced carrots
- 1 Tbsp chopped arugula or 2 Tbsp chopped fresh parsley
- 2 bay leaves
- 4 cups well-flavored vegetable stock
- Salt and ground black pepper
- Light cream, to serve

Preparation: 15 minutes
Cooking time: 30 minutes

❶ Cook the onion in the oil until softened but not browned, then add the pumpkin and carrots, and continue cooking for about 5 minutes. Stir in the lovage or parsley, bay leaves, and stock, then bring the soup gradually to a boil. Season well, then cover the pan, and simmer for 30 minutes, until all the vegetables are tender.

❷ Allow the soup to cool slightly, then remove the bay leaves, and blend until smooth in a blender or food processor. Return the soup to the pan, and stir in a little extra stock to thin the soup, if necessary. Season again, reheat gently, then serve with a generous swirl of cream.

Baked Gem Squash with Parmesan Cream

Gem squash are tiny, the jewels of the pumpkin world. Baked with a rich mixture of cream, Parmesan, and garlic, they make the most wonderful but simple appetizer.

SERVES 4

- 4 gem squash, halved and deseeded
- Olive oil
- 1¼ cups light cream
- 1¼ cups freshly shredded Parmesan cheese
- 1 mild green chile, deseeded and chopped fine
- 1–2 garlic cloves, crushed
- Pinch of ground mace (optional)
- Salt and ground black pepper

Preparation: 10 minutes
Cooking time: 30 minutes

❶ Preheat a 400°F oven. Score the flesh of the squash deeply, then drizzle with olive oil. Mix the cream with the cheese, and all the remaining ingredients, then pour the mixture into the squashes.

❷ Bake for 30 minutes, until the squash is tender. Serve immediately with a salad leaf and tomato garnish.

soups, appetizers, & relishes

Baked Gem Squash with Parmesan Cream

Baked Limed Zucchini in Cream

Limes and zucchini are very amenable partners. This is almost a savory baked custard—a crème caramel without the sugar topping.

SERVES 4

- ⅔ cup light cream
- 2 kaffir lime leaves, shredded
- 2 cups shredded green zucchini
- Grated rind and juice of 1 lime
- 1 garlic clove, crushed
- Freshly grated nutmeg
- 1 large egg, beaten
- Salt and ground black pepper
- 2 Tbsp toasted bread crumbs

Preparation: 35 minutes

Cooking time: 35 minutes

❶ Heat the cream with the lime leaves in a small saucepan or in a jug in the microwave until hot but not boiling. Leave for 20 minutes to infuse, then remove the lime leaves.

❷ Preheat a 325°F oven. Mix all the ingredients together with the flavored cream, then divide the mixture among four buttered ramekin dishes. Place the ramekins in a small roasting pan, then half fill the pan with boiling water. Bake the creams for 30 to 35 minutes.

❸ Remove the creams from the roasting pan and let cool for 5 minutes. Scatter toasted crumbs over each ramekin, then serve warm.

Melon with Figs and Prosciutto

Do I like ripe, juicy figs best with melon, or is my favorite accompaniment wafer-thin slices of moist prosciutto? I can never decide—so I have both! This "arrangement" is easy to achieve.

SERVES 4

- 12 thin slices of ripe fragrant melon, such as Charentais or cantaloupe
- 8–12 wafer-thin slices prosciutto
- 4 ripe figs
- Spanish olive oil (optional)
- Ground black pepper
- Fresh cilantro, to garnish

Preparation: 15 minutes

❶ Fan out the melon on individual plates, arranging the ham over the slices or interleaving them.

❷ Cut the figs into four—but not quite through to the base—then push slightly upward from the base to open. Add the figs to the plates.

❸ Drizzle just a little olive oil over the whole arrangement. Season the ham and fig with pepper, then garnish with cilantro before serving.

TIP

Do not chill this appetizer as the luxurious flavors will be stifled by the cold. Also, only set the ham out when you are ready to serve, as it dries out very quickly. The melon and the fig, however, may be prepared in advance, and the dish is finished in just about a minute or two.

soups, appetizers, & relishes

Pumpkin, Bacon, and Tomato Skewers

A light but very tasty appetizer of orange pumpkin and bacon—always a winning combination—with tomatoes and Parmesan cheese. Serve on a bed of rice to make a slightly more substantial dish, but a bed of dressed salad leaves is all that is really necessary. This also makes an excellent light lunch for two.

SERVES 4

FOR THE MARINADE

- 3 Tbsp extra virgin olive oil
- 1 garlic clove, crushed
- 1 Tbsp chopped fresh rosemary
- 1 tsp balsamic vinegar
- Salt and ground black pepper

- 3 x ¾-in slices orange pumpkin, deseeded and peeled
- 6 slices bacon
- 18 small tomatoes (baby plums are ideal)
- 2–3 Tbsp freshly shredded Parmesan cheese
- Dressed salad leaves, to serve

Preparation: 45 minutes
Cooking time: 8–10 minutes

❶ Mix all the ingredients for the marinade together in a shallow dish. Cut the pumpkin into ½-inch pieces, then add to the dish, tossing it in the marinade. Leave for at least 30 minutes.

❷ Preheat the broiler. Stretch the bacon, then cut the slices in half lengthwise, and roll them up. Thread the pumpkin, bacon, and tomatoes onto thin metal skewers, then brush with any remaining marinade. Broil for 6 to 8 minutes, turning occasionally, until the pumpkin is tender and the bacon is browned.

❸ Scatter the shredded cheese over the skewers as soon as they are cooked, so that it melts.

❹ Serve the skewers on a bed of dressed salad leaves.

soups, appetizers, & relishes

Roast Crown Prince Squash and Pistachio Pâté

This really is one of my favorite recipes for squash. I don't miss meat, liver, or fish in this thick pâté because the flavor and texture of the squash is wonderful. And it's so easy to make!

SERVES 6

- 1½ lb crown prince squash, deseeded
- Salt and ground black pepper
- Olive oil
- 1 cup cream cheese
- 1–2 garlic cloves, crushed
- 1 hot red chile, deseeded and chopped fine
- ⅓ cup pistachios, chopped

Preparation: 1½ hours
Chilling time: 30 minutes

❶ Preheat a 425°F oven. Cut the squash into 1-in slices. Place them in a roasting pan, and season lightly. Drizzle with olive oil, then roast for 45 minutes. Leave the squash to cool, then cut the flesh away from the skin and mash it roughly.

❷ Beat the cream cheese with the garlic and chile until smooth. Add the squash, mix together, then add the nuts, and season well. Turn into a serving dish and chill for 30 minutes.

❸ Serve piled on hot toasts with a garnish of arugula leaves.

Curried Lamb and Pumpkin Koftas

Koftas are a cross between meatballs and kabobs, a meat mixture molded onto skewers and then barbecued or broiled. I often mold the same mixture into baby patties and broil them, as this saves time.

SERVES 4

- 1 onion, chopped
- 1 garlic clove
- 1 Tbsp curry powder
- 1–2 red chiles, chopped (optional)
- 1 green bell pepper, deseeded and chopped
- 1 Tbsp oil
- 1 lb 2 oz ground lamb
- 1 cup thick pumpkin purée, fresh or canned
- Salt
- 1 cup fresh whole wheat bread crumbs
- Oil, for cooking

Preparation: 25–30 minutes
Cooking time: 10 minutes

❶ Blend the onion, garlic, curry powder, chiles, and bell pepper in a blender or food processor until smooth.

❷ Heat the oil in a large frying pan, add the lamb, and cook quickly until browned all over, stirring frequently to break up any lumps of meat that form. Add the onion paste, cook for 2 to 3 minutes, then stir in the pumpkin, and cook until it is heated through. Season to taste with the salt.

❸ Remove the pan from the heat and stir in the bread crumbs to give a slightly moist but moldable mixture. Allow to cool, then shape into 12 to 15 patties or mold around wooden skewers. Broil the koftas for 3 to 4 minutes on each side, brushing them from time to time with a little oil if necessary to keep them moist.

❹ Serve with a spoonful of rice or some salad leaves, and a yogurt dip—the cucumber and radish raita on page 34 would be ideal.

Spiced Minted Melon Balls

A spiced vinaigrette is the perfect foil for the sweetness of a melon that you wish to serve as a starter. Serve at room temperature and not chilled—too cold, and the melon will have little flavor, even if really ripe.

SERVES 4

- ½ tsp cumin seeds
- ½ ripe melon, such as cantaloupe, Galia, or honeydew
- ½ medium cucumber, peeled and diced fine
- 3 tomatoes, deseeded and diced
- 3 Tbsp finely chopped fresh mint
- Salt and sugar
- 3 Tbsp light olive oil
- 1 Tbsp white wine vinegar
- Mint sprigs, to garnish

Preparation: 30 minutes

Marinating time: 30 minutes

❶ Heat a small frying pan over medium heat, add the cumin seeds, and toast them for just 30 seconds, until fragrant. Turn out of the pan and allow the seeds to cool.

❷ Scoop the melon into balls and place them in a bowl with the cucumber and tomatoes. Sprinkle the chopped mint with a little salt and sugar to bring out its flavor.

❸ Whisk together the oil, vinegar, and mint. Grind the cumin seeds using a pestle and mortar or with the end of a rolling pin, then add them to the dressing, with salt and sugar to taste. Pour the dressing over the salad and let stand for 30 minutes. Serve in small dishes, garnished with sprigs of mint.

Pumpkin Chutney

If you buy a pumpkin in October to make chutney in December or January, do turn the pumpkin every day or so, to stop moisture collecting inside.

MAKES ABOUT 3 LB

- 2 lb 4 oz peeled, seeded, and diced pumpkin flesh
- 2 onions, chopped fine
- 1 Tbsp salt, plus 2 tsp
- 1 lb 2 oz fresh tomatoes, skinned, if you prefer, and chopped
- ⅔ cup golden raisins
- 2 cups light brown sugar
- 1½ Tbsp ground ginger
- 2 garlic cloves, crushed
- 1½ cups white wine or distilled malt vinegar

Preparation: 15 minutes

+ 2 hours standing

Cooking time: 1 hour

❶ Mix the pumpkin and onion together, then add 1 tablespoon salt, stir well, and leave for 2 hours. Drain and rinse well.

❷ Turn into a large preserving pan and add the remaining ingredients. Bring slowly to a boil, stirring all the time, then simmer for about 45 minutes, until reduced and thickened.

❸ Spoon into warm screw-top jars. Store for a month or more.

Pumpkin Chutney

Butternut and Chicken Liver Pâté

Meat or liver-only pâtés can make a very rich prelude to a meal. Mix some garlic-flavored livers with roasted butternut squash, and the resulting pâté is lighter, and, even better, it goes further too! Using low-fat cream cheese helps to keep the calories and the richness of the pâté under control.

SERVES 6–8

- 1 butternut squash (weighing about 1 lb 9 oz–1 lb 12 oz)
- Salt and ground black pepper
- Olive oil
- 1 small onion, chopped fine
- 1 garlic clove, crushed
- 14 oz chicken livers
- 1 Tbsp fresh thyme leaves
- 1 cup low-fat cream cheese
- Thyme, paprika, or melted butter, to garnish

Preparation and cooking time:
1 hour
Chilling time: 2 hours

---

❶ Preheat a 425°F oven. Cut the squash in half lengthwise, scoop out the seeds, then arrange the halves in a small roasting pan. Season lightly, then drizzle with olive oil. Roast for 30 to 35 minutes, until the flesh is tender, then leave to cool.

❷ Heat 3 tablespoons of olive oil in a large frying pan, then add the onion, and cook for 3 to 4 minutes until starting to soften. Add the garlic and chicken livers with the thyme, then cook over high heat for 3 to 4 minutes, until the livers are cooked through and lightly browned. Remove the pan from the heat and allow to cool.

❸ Scrape the cream cheese into the bowl of a blender or food processor and add the chicken liver mixture with the flesh of the butternut squash. Blend until smooth, then add seasonings to taste.

❹ Scrape the pâté into a serving bowl and smooth the top. Chill for 2 hours, then garnish with a sprig of thyme or paprika before serving. You could seal the top of the pâté with melted butter if you wish, which you should then allow to set for 30 minutes in the fridge. Serve the pâté with lots of fresh toast, and a salad garnish, if you wish.

soups, appetizers, & relishes

Pumpkin Relish

This Norwegian recipe keeps well, and is utterly delicious—a surprising mixture of sweet and savory.

MAKES 3–4 LBS.

- ½ medium orange pumpkin
- About 2¼ cups white wine vinegar
- About 2¼ cups water

Preparation: 20 minutes or overnight

Cooking time: 1 hour 15 minutes

---

❶ Deseed and peel the pumpkin, then cut the flesh into ½-inch dice. Place in a large bowl, cover with equal parts white wine vinegar and water, then cover, and leave for 8 hours or overnight.

❷ Drain the pumpkin and then weigh it. To each 2 lb 4 oz of pumpkin, add 5½ cups sugar, 1 cup white wine vinegar, ¼ cup chopped fresh ginger root.

❸ Mix the ingredients together in a large preserving pan, then bring slowly to a boil. Boil gently for 30 to 40 minutes, until the pumpkin is just soft, then scoop it out of the pan with a slotted spoon and pack into warmed glass jars. Pour over the slightly reduced syrup, then seal the jars loosely. Check the relish after 4 or 5 hours, top up with extra syrup if necessary, then seal properly. Keep in a cool place. and leave for a few weeks before eating.

Cucumber and Radish Raita

Cucumber raita has saved my palate several times when a curry has turned out hotter than planned!

SERVES 4 AS AN ACCOMPANIMENT

- 1 Tbsp white mustard seeds
- 1 Tbsp cumin seeds
- ½ medium cucumber
- ½ cup red radishes, chopped fine
- 1 cup plain yogurt
- Salt and ground black pepper
- 2 Tbsp chopped fresh cilantro
- Chili powder, to garnish

Preparation: 10 minutes

---

❶ Heat a frying pan over medium heat until hot, add the mustard and cumin seeds, and fry for not more than 1 minute, until the spices are fragrant and starting to brown. Turn out into a mortar or on to a chopping board and allow to cool slightly, then crush the seeds with a pestle or the end of a rolling pin.

❷ Grate the cucumber coarsely— this is easiest to do in a blender or food processor—then squeeze the strands dry in your hands. Turn into a bowl, then add the spices, radishes, and yogurt. Mix well, adding seasonings to taste, then add the cilantro.

❸ Sprinkle the raita with chili powder just before serving—not too much, though, as this is meant to be cooling, after all! (For a picture of this recipe, see page 105, Pumpkin and Okra Curry.)

soups, appetizers, & relishes

Roasted Pumpkin, Tomato, and Eggplant Salad

Roast Squash, Vegetable, and Pasta Salad

Melon, Grape, and Chicken Salad

Cucumber Salad with Spiced Pork and Sesame Seeds

Pasta Salad Verde

Warm Roasted Pumpkin and Green Bean Salad

Warm Mushroom and Patty Pan Salad

Belgian Endive, Tomato, and Melon Salad

Gem Squash Salad

Roasted Bell Pepper and Squash Salad

Spiced Zucchini and Roasted Squash Salad

Squash, Cucumber, and Bulgur Wheat Salad

Chili Bean and Pumpkin Salad

Zucchini and Squash Ratatouille with Melon

Pumpkin and Spinach Salad with Feta Cheese

Roasted Pumpkin, Tomato, and Eggplant Salad

Complementary flavors that pack a punch! Serve this salad warm or cold, on a bed of arugula leaves, with plenty of Italian flat bread.

SERVES 4

- 8 slices from a small pumpkin, each about ¾-in thick, deseeded
- 1 eggplant, quartered lengthwise
- 2 large slicing tomatoes, halved
- 6–8 garlic cloves, unpeeled
- Salt and ground black pepper
- 6–8 basil leaves, torn in half
- Sugar
- Olive oil
- Basil leaves, to garnish
- Olive oil bread, to serve

FOR THE DRESSING

- 6 Tbsp extra virgin olive oil
- 1 Tbsp balsamic or sherry vinegar
- 1 tsp Dijon mustard
- Pinch of sugar
- 1 tsp chopped arugula or 1 Tbsp chopped fresh parsley

Preparation: 20 minutes
Cooking time: 45 minutes
---

❶ Preheat a 425°F oven. Arrange the prepared vegetables with the garlic in a roasting pan, then season with salt and pepper. Push the basil leaves into the flesh of the tomatoes, then scatter over a little sugar. Drizzle everything with olive oil, then roast at the top of the oven for 40–45 minutes, until the vegetables are just starting to blacken. (Check after 30 minutes and remove the tomatoes if they are already soft.)

❷ Allow the vegetables to cool slightly, then cut the pumpkin away from the skin. Leave for 10 minutes, if you intend to serve the salad warm, or until completely cold.

❸ Prepare the dressing by blending all the ingredients together and season with salt, pepper, and sugar to taste.

❹ Peel the garlic, then arrange the vegetables on serving plates. Pour the dressing over and then add a little fresh basil to each helping. Serve immediately with plenty of olive oil bread.

salads

Roast Squash, Vegetable, and Pasta Salad

A filling salad that you can enjoy either as a main course, or in smaller quantities as an appetizer.

SERVES 4 AS A MAIN COURSE,
6–8 AS AN APPETIZER

- 4 x 1-in slices crown prince squash, deseeded
- 2 yellow zucchini, trimmed
- 1 large eggplant, halved lengthwise
- 1 large red bell pepper
- 1 garlic bulb
- Salt and ground black pepper
- Olive oil
- 7 oz fresh or dried tagliatelli, spaghetti, or other noodles

FOR THE DRESSING

- 6 Tbsp extra virgin olive oil
- 2 Tbsp balsamic vinegar
- 1 tsp Dijon mustard
- Sugar
- Mixed salad leaves, to serve

Preparation: 30 minutes

Cooking time: 40 minutes

---

❶ Preheat a 425°F oven. Place all the vegetables in a roasting pan, season lightly, and drizzle with olive oil. Roast for 40 minutes, or until they are tender and beginning to blacken. Turn the zucchini, bell pepper, and eggplant during cooking, and remove the vegetables as they are done.

❷ Cover the bell peppers with a damp cloth as soon as they come out of the oven, then leave all the vegetables to cool. Peel the skins away from the bell peppers, then remove their cores and seeds.

❸ Blend all the ingredients for the vinaigrette together and season well to taste. Cook the pasta, drain in a colander and shake briefly, then turn into a glass serving dish, and add half the vinaigrette. Toss, then leave to cool completely.

❹ Peel the squash, then chop the roasted vegetables into bite-size pieces, and squeeze the garlic cloves from their skins. Pile the vegetables over the pasta, top with the salad leaves and pour over the remaining dressing. Toss just before serving.

Melon, Grape, and Chicken Salad

A very filling salad comprising a wonderful mélange of ingredients. I like to use dolcelatte in the dressing, a slightly sweet cheese that draws out the flavors of the melon and grapes. Any crumbly blue would be a good alternative.

SERVES 2

- Mixed salad leaves
- 2 small cooked chicken breasts, skinned and boned
- ½ ripe melon, such as piel de sapo, Galia, cantaloupe, or honeydew, scooped into balls
- 4 scallions, chopped
- 2 tomatoes, deseeded and chopped
- 1 mild red chile, deseeded and chopped fine
- ¼ medium cucumber, diced
- ½ cup small seedless black grapes
- Salt and ground black pepper

FOR THE DRESSING
- 3 Tbsp mayonnaise
- ¼ cup crumbled blue-veined cheese
- Paprika, to garnish

Preparation: 15–20 minutes

❶ Arrange the salad leaves on two serving plates. Slice the chicken, then arrange on the leaves.

❷ Combine all the remaining salad ingredients and season well. Spoon over the chicken, drizzling any juices from the melon over the meat.

❸ Mix the mayonnaise with the crumbled cheese, and season lightly, then dollop a spoonful of dressing on top of each portion.

❹ Sprinkle with paprika then serve immediately.

salads

Cucumber Salad with Spiced Pork and Sesame Seeds

A real main course of a salad, combining hot meat and vegetables with the crispness of salad leaves. The subtle spicing and the sesame seeds add extra interest.

SERVES 4

- 1 small head Bok choy, shredded
- 1 medium cucumber, deseeded and diced
- 1 red bell pepper, deseeded and sliced
- 3 Tbsp peanut oil
- 1 pork fillet (weighing about 1 lb 2 oz), trimmed and sliced thin
- 1 tsp chili sauce, or more according to taste
- 1 eggplant, sliced thin
- 1 red onion, sliced thin

- 1 garlic clove, sliced
- 1 green bell pepper, deseeded and sliced
- 2 Tbsp light soy sauce
- 2 Tbsp sesame seeds

Preparation: 15 minutes

Cooking time: 10 minutes
---

❶ Arrange the Bok choy and cucumber in a large salad bowl with the red bell pepper, then leave in a cool place until required.

❷ Heat the oil in a large frying pan or wok, then add the pork fillet, and cook quickly to brown. Add the chili sauce, then the eggplant, and stir-fry until the eggplant is beginning to brown. Add the remaining vegetables, and stir-fry briefly, then add the soy sauce. Scatter the sesame seeds into the pan, stir, then spoon the meat and vegetables over the prepared salad leaves. Toss lightly, then serve immediately.

salads

40

Pasta Salad Verde

The secret of a really tasty salad is in the dressing. A healthy low-calorie vinaigrette simply will not do.

SERVES 4–6
- 9 oz tricolored pasta shapes, such as fusilli
- 2 Tbsp extra virgin olive oil
- 4 large scallions, chopped fine
- 2 zucchini, cut into julienne strips
- ½ medium cucumber, deseeded and diced
- 1½ cups young spinach leaves, sliced fine

FOR THE DRESSING
- 1 large ripe avocado, peeled and chopped
- Juice of 1 lemon
- ½ cup mayonnaise
- ½ cup unsweetened yogurt
- 1 garlic clove, crushed
- ¾ cup crumbled blue cheese
- 1 mild green chile, deseeded and chopped

Preparation: 20 minutes
Cooking time: 15 minutes

❶ Bring a large pan of salted water to a boil, then add the pasta, and cook according to instructions. Drain, then turn the pasta into a bowl, and add the olive oil. Toss so that all the pasta is coated.

❷ Add all the prepared vegetables to the cold pasta, mix well, and season. Mash the avocado with the lemon juice. Add the remaining dressing ingredients, and blend well. Season to taste. Spoon on the dressing.

Warm Roasted Pumpkin and Green Bean Salad

A colorful combination that tastes really good! I like the contrasts between the vegetable shapes too.

SERVES 4
- 4 x 1-in slices orange pumpkin, deseeded
- Salt and ground black pepper
- Olive oil
- 1 large onion, chopped fine
- 1 garlic clove, sliced fine
- 14-oz can chopped tomatoes
- 1½ cups green beans, cut into 1-in lengths
- 8–10 fresh basil leaves, roughly torn

Preparation: 1 hour
Cooking time: 15 minutes

❶ Preheat a 425°F oven. Place the pumpkin in a small roasting pan, season lightly, and drizzle with olive oil. Roast the pumpkin for 40 to 45 minutes, or until tender.

❷ Meanwhile, prepare the sauce. Cook the onion in 2 tablespoons olive oil for about 5 minutes, until softened but not browned. Add the garlic and tomatoes, bring to a boil, then stir in the beans. Simmer for 8 to 10 minutes, until the beans are just tender, then season to taste.

❸ Peel the roasted pumpkin and cut into 1-inch chunks. Add to the beans and tomatoes, then allow to cool slightly. Add the basil, then serve warm.

salads

41

Warm Mushroom and Patty Pan Salad

This salad can be turned into something really special by combining baby patty pan squash with a selection of mixed mushrooms.

SERVES 4

- Mixed salad leaves, to serve
- 2 Tbsp oil
- 1 lb 2 oz baby patty pan squashes, topped and tailed
- 3 cups mixed, wild mushrooms such as chestnut, shiitake, and oyster, sliced
- 2 garlic cloves, sliced fine
- 4 halves sun-dried tomatoes in oil, shredded, or 6 anchovy fillets, chopped
- 1–2 Tbsp balsamic vinegar
- Salt and ground black pepper
- Shavings of fresh Parmesan cheese, to serve (optional)

Preparation: 10–15 minutes
Cooking time: 8 minutes

❶ Arrange the salad leaves on four serving plates. Heat a large frying pan or wok until hot, then add the oil. Add the squashes and stir-fry for 2 minutes, then stir in the mushrooms and garlic, and continue to fry for 2 to 3 minutes until the squashes are just tender. Stir in the shredded tomatoes or chopped anchovies.

❷ Arrange the colorful squash and mushroom mixture over the salad leaves.

❸ Add the vinegar to the pan juices, bring to a boil, then season to taste. Pour the dressing over the salad and serve immediately, garnished with a little fresh Parmesan if you wish.

Gem Squash Salad

A great appetizer or supper dish, lightly chilled gem squash are filled with a crisp salad stuffing. Use four to six slices of prosciutto in place of roasted ham if you prefer.

SERVES 2

- 2 gem squash
- 1 little gem lettuce, torn into small pieces
- ¾ cup cold, cooked, diced potato
- 6 cherry tomatoes, halved
- 2 scallions, sliced fine
- 1 small carrot, cut into fine julienne strips or shredded fine
- 1 mild red chile, deseeded and chopped fine (optional)
- 2 slices roasted ham, shredded fine
- Salt and ground black pepper
- 1 Tbsp chopped fresh parsley
- 2–3 Tbsp mayonnaise or vinaigrette

Preparation: 15 minutes
Cooking time: 25 minutes
---

❶ Pierce the squash two or three times with a fork. Cook in a large pan of boiling water for 20 to 25 minutes, then drain, and leave to cool. Cut away the tops of the squash then scoop out and discard the seeds. Score the remaining flesh to make it easier to scoop out with a spoon, then rub a little oil over the shells to make them shine.

❷ Mix all the remaining ingredients together, binding them lightly with a little mayonnaise or vinaigrette.

❸ Pile the filling into the squash, then arrange any extra in the base of individual serving bowls. Place the squash on top. Chill lightly.

Belgian Endive, Tomato, and Melon Salad

A sweet and yet savory salad, and one which makes a perfect accompaniment to any spicy dish, especially the Spicy Pumpkin Stuffed Cod on page 56. Use tiny whole or halved tomatoes.

SERVES 4

- 2 large heads Belgian endive, broken into leaves
- 4 ripe tomatoes, deseeded and chopped
- 2–3 scallions, chopped fine
- 20 melon balls, cut from a ripe Galia melon
- 4–6 Tbsp mustard or garlic vinaigrette

Preparation: 10 minutes
---

❶ Break the Belgian endive into leaves and arrange on four serving plates.

❷ Chop the tomatoes then add them to the endive, along with the scallions, and melon balls.

❸ Spoon the vinaigrette over the whole arrangement and serve immediately.

salads

Gem Squash Salad

Roasted Bell Pepper and Squash Salad

Roasted bell pepper salads are very popular, and they can be varied according to the other vegetables added to them. The sweet yet savory flavor of crown prince squash makes a perfect partner.

SERVES 4

- 4 bell peppers, of mixed colors
- 1 lb 2 oz–1 lb 5 oz piece crown prince squash, deseeded and quartered
- Mixed salad leaves
- Pesto sauce to serve (optional)

FOR THE DRESSING

- 6 Tbsp extra virgin olive oil
- 2 Tbsp sherry vinegar
- 1 garlic clove, crushed

- Salt and ground black pepper
- Sugar, to taste
- 1 Tbsp torn basil leaves

Preparation: 30 minutes
Cooking time: 40 minutes
Marinating time: 30 minutes

---

❶ Preheat a 425°F oven. Place the bell peppers and squash on a baking sheet and roast for 35 to 40 minutes, until the bell peppers are blackened and blistered and the squash is tender. Turn the bell peppers over half-way through cooking.

❷ Remove the slices of squash, then cover the bell peppers with a damp dish towel and leave for 10 to 15 minutes, until cool enough to handle. Peel away the loosened skins from the bell peppers, starting at the flower end, then pull out the core and seeds.

❸ Peel the squash flesh away from the skin and cut it into small chunks. Slice the bell peppers and mix them with the squash in a bowl. Add all the ingredients for the dressing, using a pinch or two of sugar, stir well, then leave for at least 30 minutes, tossing occasionally.

❹ Serve the salad on a bed of mixed leaves, with plenty of the dressing spooned over. A little spoonful of pesto makes the perfect garnish for each helping.

TIP

Use one each red, green, yellow, and orange bell pepper for a really colorful salad.

Spiced Zucchini, and Roasted Squash Salad

Seasoned with the exotic flavorings of Morocco, this salad makes an extremely useful addition to a buffet table as it is economical to make and very filling.

SERVES 6

- 1 butternut squash (weighing about 2 lb 4 oz)
- Salt and ground black pepper
- Olive oil
- 3 cups sliced zucchini
- ½ cup pumpkin seeds, toasted if wished

FOR THE DRESSING

- 3 Tbsp olive oil
- 2 Tbsp white wine vinegar
- 1 green chile, chopped fine
- 1 tsp chili sauce
- Pinch of ground cumin
- Pinch of ground cinnamon
- 2 Tbsp chopped fresh cilantro

Preparation: 20 minutes
Cooking time: 40 minutes

❶ Preheat a 425°F oven. Cut the squash in half and scoop out the seeds, then arrange the halves in a small roasting pan. Season lightly, drizzle with olive oil, then roast for 30 to 35 minutes, or until tender.

❷ Fry the zucchini in 4 tablespoons oil until just starting to brown, but still quite firm. Scoop them out of the pan into a large salad bowl.

❸ Blend the dressing ingredients with the oil left in the pan, and season to taste.

❹ Scoop the flesh out of the skins of the squash and chop roughly. Add the squash to the zucchini, with the pumpkin seeds, and toss well, then pour the dressing over.

TIP
The flesh around the hollow of the squash is quite likely to fall apart, whereas the denser squash should stay together and cut into chunks.

salads

Squash, Cucumber, and Bulgur Wheat Salad

Tabbouleh, a mix of bulgur wheat and cucumber, with lots of chopped mint and parsley, is a traditional Middle Eastern salad which is very fashionable today. As cucumbers and squashes are related I have taken the salad one stage further and added finely diced squash to the traditional mix, along with a few nuts. I am delighted with the result.

SERVES 8

- 1 cup fine bulgur wheat
- 2 cups boiling water
- 1½ cups cucumber, diced fine
- 1½ cups diced and roasted winter squash, such as crown prince, butternut, or kabocha
- ½ cup chopped fresh parsley
- 3 Tbsp chopped arugula
- 2 tomatoes, deseeded and chopped
- 2 scallions, sliced
- ⅓ cup toasted almonds, chopped
- Juice of 1 lemon
- Salt and ground black pepper
- ¼ cup extra virgin olive oil

Preparation: 45 minutes

---

❶ Soak the bulgur wheat in the boiling water and let stand for 30 minutes. Squeeze the grains dry in a dish towel, then turn them into a large salad bowl.

❷ Add all the remaining ingredients, with plenty of seasoning to taste. Toss the salad well, then serve at room temperature.

salads

Chili Bean and Pumpkin Salad

A Tex-Mex salad which will really fill you up! Add some cooked chicken, or even some flakes of smoked mackerel, to the salad if you wish, but it makes an excellent lunch or supper dish as it is.

SERVES 4

- 2 cups chopped, cooked pumpkin
- 1 tsp chili powder
- Pinch of ground cumin
- 3 Tbsp olive oil
- 1 Romaine lettuce, or 2–3 little gems, torn into bite-size pieces
- 14-oz can red kidney beans, drained
- 4 scallions, chopped fine
- 4 fresh tomatoes, deseeded and chopped
- 1 large ripe avocado, peeled and chopped
- Grated rind and juice of 1 lime
- 1 mild green chile, deseeded and chopped
- Salt and ground black pepper
- 4 Tbsp vinaigrette
- Tortilla chips, to serve

Preparation: 15 minutes

Cooking time: 5 minutes

❶ Toss the cooked pumpkin in the chili powder and cumin, then stir-fry briefly in the oil in a large frying pan until lightly browned. Cook over medium or low heat, or the spices will burn. Allow to cool.

❷ Arrange the lettuce in the base of a salad bowl. Combine the spiced squash with all the remaining ingredients, except the tortilla chips, and pile over the lettuce. Top with the chips, then serve immediately.

TIP

Cook your own kidney beans if you like, but canned beans make this a very quick salad to prepare.

Zucchini and Squash Ratatouille with Melon

This is a most unusual and delicious ratatouille. I have replaced the traditional eggplant with squash, and added some melon balls just before serving— the flavors and texture are excellent. I have used a honeydew melon for a contrast in color, but a watermelon would also work well.

SERVES 8

- 1 large onion, sliced
- 2 cups diced winter squash, such as butternut or crown prince
- 4 Tbsp olive oil
- 2 zucchini, sliced thick
- 1 green bell pepper, diced
- 2–3 plump garlic cloves, sliced fine
- 2 x 14-oz cans chopped tomatoes
- Salt and ground black pepper
- 1 Tbsp chopped arugula or 2–3 Tbsp torn fresh basil leaves
- 2–3 cups honeydew melon balls

Preparation: 20 minutes
Cooking time: 20–25 minutes

❶ Cook the onion and squash in the oil until the squash is starting to brown, then add the zucchini, bell pepper, and garlic, and cook for 5 minutes more.

❷ Add the chopped tomatoes, salt, and pepper, and bring to a boil. Simmer for about 10 minutes, or until the sauce has thickened but the vegetables still retain their texture.

❸ Season the ratatouille to taste then leave to cool. Add the arugula or basil and melon balls just before serving at room temperature.

Pumpkin and Spinach Salad with Feta Cheese

The soft texture and slightly sweet flavor of either pumpkin or squash combines very well with young spinach leaves, tomatoes, and crumbly feta cheese to make a salad that will wake up your taste buds.

SERVES 4

- ¼ cup pine nuts
- 4 good handfuls young spinach leaves
- 1 cup loosely packed arugula leaves
- 2 large tomatoes, sliced thin, or 24 baby plum or cherry tomatoes
- 1½ cups diced cooked pumpkin
- 1 cup diced feta cheese
- Salt and ground black pepper
- Extra virgin olive oil

Preparation: 10 minutes

---

❶ Heat a frying pan until hot, then add the pine nuts, and stir-fry for 1 to 2 minutes, until lightly golden. Scoop the nuts out of the pan and leave to cool.

❷ Arrange the spinach and arugula leaves on a serving platter or individual plates, then top with the tomatoes, squash, and cheese. Scatter the toasted pine nuts over, then season the salad lightly with salt and pepper.

❸ Drizzle with the olive oil just before serving.

TIP

The pumpkin and feta cheese should both be cut into equal-size diced chunks.

Shrimp and Zucchini Lasagna

Squash with Shrimp

Crab, Almond, and Pumpkin Curry

Roast Monkfish and Pumpkin with Rice

Zucchini and Fresh Tuna Risotto

Spicy Pumpkin Stuffed Cod

Broiled Sardines with Spaghetti Squash

Hot Chili Haddock with Spaghetti Squash

Pumpkin Plaice with Zucchini Sauce

Mixed Fish Cakes with Zucchini Salad

Fisherman's Pumpkin Pie

Mussels and Squash with Tomato Spaghetti

Squash and Zucchini Trout

Broiled Mackerel with Apple and Cucumber Salsa

Scallops with Baby Patty Pans and Bacon

Squid and Pumpkin Stew with Tomatoes

Fish Dishes

Shrimp and Zucchini Lasagna

I add lots of shredded raw zucchini to this lasagna before cooking, which gives a good texture to the dish. Leave the tomato sauce quite wet as the pasta will need the extra moisture to cook tender.

SERVES 4

- 1 onion, chopped fine
- 2 Tbsp olive oil
- 1 garlic clove, crushed
- 1 Tbsp fresh thyme leaves
- ½ cup dry white wine
- 14-oz can chopped tomatoes
- Salt and ground black pepper
- 3 cups shredded zucchini
- 14 oz large peeled shrimp
- 2 cups plain yogurt
- ½ cup crumbled goat cheese, with or without herbs
- 10–12 sheets fresh or no-precook lasagna

Preparation: 30 minutes
Cooking time: 30 minutes

---

❶ Preheat a 400°F oven. Lightly butter a suitably sized ovenproof gratin dish.

❷ Cook the onion in the oil until softened but not browned, then add the garlic and thyme. Add the wine, then cook quickly until it has almost evaporated. Stir in the chopped tomatoes, with some seasoning, then stir in the zucchini and shrimp.

❸ Beat the yogurt and goat cheese together, and add a little seasoning to taste.

❹ Spoon half the zucchini and shrimp mixture into the buttered dish, then cover with a layer of lasagna. Repeat the layers, then finish by spooning the cheese mixture over the top.

❺ Bake the lasagna for 30 minutes, or until the topping is golden brown. Serve immediately.

Squash with Shrimp

This recipe has long been a favorite of mine, and is one that I adapted from an idea for sweet potatoes. The smoked bacon and squash give wonderful background flavors to the garlic-fried shrimp. Serve the dish with a little plain boiled rice—the squash is starchy, so you won't need much extra carbohydrate—and a large, crisp green salad or plenty of steamed vegetables.

SERVES 4

- 1 lb 9 oz peeled, seeded crown prince squash, cut into 1-in chunks
- 5 Tbsp extra virgin olive oil
- 4 slices smoked bacon, diced
- 1¼ cups well-flavored vegetable stock
- 3–4 sprigs fresh thyme
- 2 bay leaves
- Salt and ground black pepper
- ½ stick butter
- 20 large unpeeled shrimp, raw or cooked
- 1–2 plump garlic cloves, crushed
- 3 Tbsp white wine vinegar
- Fresh thyme leaves, to garnish

Preparation: 15 minutes
Cooking time: 30 minutes

❶ Cook the squash in the oil in a large frying pan for about 10 minutes, until starting to soften and brown, adding the diced bacon after 5 minutes. Then add the stock, herbs, and seasoning, and bring to a boil. Cover and cook for 10 to 15 minutes, until the squash is just tender, then remove the bay leaves and thyme.

❷ Meanwhile, melt the butter in a separate frying pan, add the shrimp and garlic, and toss in the butter. Cook for 2 to 3 minutes until the shrimp are hot, or until pink and cooked through if using raw.

❸ Add the shrimp and their juices to the squash with the vinegar, toss gently over the heat, and adjust the seasoning if necessary. Serve immediately, garnished with fresh thyme leaves.

fish dishes

55

Crab, Almond, and Pumpkin Curry

A rich, mild curry to serve on a very special occasion. Increase the spiciness if you wish by adding a chopped chile or two, but do not drown out the flavor of the crab and squash. Use a mixture of white and brown meats for the best flavor, or canned white crab meat if you prefer. Serve the curry with rice, or Indian flat breads.

SERVES 4

- 1 onion, chopped
- 1–2 garlic cloves, chopped
- 2-in piece fresh ginger root, peeled and chopped
- 1 Tbsp mild curry powder
- 3 Tbsp peanut oil
- 3 Tbsp whole blanched almonds
- 1 cup peeled, seeded, and diced pumpkin
- ¾ cup milk
- ⅔ cup light cream
- 10½ oz prepared crab meat
- Salt
- 2–3 Tbsp chopped fresh cilantro

Preparation: 15 minutes
Cooking time: 12–15 minutes

---

❶ Blend the onion, garlic, ginger, and curry powder until smooth in a blender or food processor. Heat the oil in a large frying pan, add the almonds, and cook for 2 to 3 minutes, until golden brown. Scoop the nuts out of the oil with a slotted spoon and set aside.

❷ Add the diced pumpkin to the oil and cook over medium-high heat for 3 to 4 minutes, until starting to soften and brown, then add the curry paste. Lower the heat and cook for 5 minutes, stirring frequently.

❸ Stir the milk and cream into the curry, then add the crab meat with the almonds. Season lightly with salt, then heat gently until the crab meat is piping hot. Stir in the cilantro, and serve immediately.

Roast Monkfish and Pumpkin with Rice

Instead of serving this dish on a bed of rice, use it as a filling for flour tortillas for a change. Both ideas are equally delicious.

SERVES 4

- 20 x 1-in dice (8oz) peeled, seeded pumpkin
- 8 large tomatoes, halved
- 2 garlic cloves
- 1 small onion, quartered
- 2 mild red chiles, halved and deseeded
- 3–4 large sprigs fresh basil
- 3–4 sprigs fresh oregano
- Salt and ground black pepper
- Sugar
- Olive oil
- 1 large monkfish tail (weighing 1 lb 2 oz–1 lb 5 oz)
- 1½ cups long grain rice
- Fresh basil sprigs, to garnish

Preparation: 15 minutes
Cooking time: 40 minutes

❶ Preheat a 425°F oven. Arrange the prepared pumpkin at one end of a small roasting pan, then add the tomatoes, garlic, onion, and chiles at the other end. Tuck the fresh herbs amongst the tomatoes. Season all the vegetables with salt and pepper, scatter the tomatoes with a little sugar, then drizzle everything with olive oil. Roast for 30 minutes, or until the pumpkin is tender and everything is just starting to blacken.

❷ Trim the monkfish tail and remove any skin. Season lightly, then place in a suitable baking dish and drizzle with olive oil. Roast with the vegetables for 15 to 20 minutes, until just cooked.

❸ Meanwhile, cook the rice according to the instructions.

❹ Remove the pumpkin from the roasting pan. To make the coulis, blend the remaining vegetables in a blender or food processor. Press the resulting paste through a sieve with the back of a ladle, then season according to taste.

❺ Strain the rice, if necessary, and arrange on four warmed plates. Cut the monkfish fillets away from the bone, then slice the fish thickly. Arrange the monkfish with the pumpkin over the rice, then spoon the coulis over. Garnish with the fresh basil and serve with steamed green vegetables or a tossed green salad, if you wish.

fish dishes

57

Zucchini and Fresh Tuna Risotto

When there is a glut of zucchini in the garden we often make a risotto or spaghetti dish flavored with just zucchini, garlic, and fresh Parmesan cheese. However, some fresh tuna, marinated in lime, olive oil, and garlic, will turn a very simple dish into a splendid feast.

Serves 4

- 1 lb 2 oz fresh tuna, cut into 1-in pieces
- Grated rind and juice of 2 limes
- 2 garlic cloves, crushed
- 6 Tbsp olive oil
- Salt and ground black pepper
- 1 large onion, chopped fine
- 1½ cups arborio rice
- 5 cups well-flavored fish or vegetable stock
- 4 cups shredded zucchini
- Shavings of fresh Parmesan cheese, to garnish

Preparation: 10 minutes
+ marinating time
Cooking time: 25 minutes

---

❶ Place the tuna in a suitable glass dish, then add the grated lime rind and juice, 1 garlic clove, and 3 tablespoons olive oil, with a little seasoning. Stir well, then cover, and leave in a cool place for at least 1 hour, or up to a day. (If you leave the fish for around 24 hours, it will be almost pickled, and require very little cooking.)

❷ Cook the onion in the remaining oil in a large frying pan for 4 to 5 minutes, until soft but not browned. Add the rice, and toss it in the pan juices, then stir in about one third of the stock. Bring to a boil, then cook until all the stock has been absorbed, stirring frequently. Add half the remaining stock and repeat the cooking process.

❸ Add the tuna and its marinade to the pan, and cook for 2 to 3 minutes, then add the remaining stock, and continue as before. Stir the shredded zucchini into the pan with the remaining garlic for the last 2 to 3 minutes of the cooking time, when the stock has almost all been absorbed.

❹ Season the risotto to taste, then serve with a tomato salad, if you wish, garnishing the risotto with shavings of fresh Parmesan cheese.

Tip

The easiest and most efficient way to shred zucchini is in a blender or food processor.

fish dishes

Spicy Pumpkin Stuffed Cod

You will need really fresh cod fillet for this recipe, so that the flavor of the fish is not overpowered by the strength of the filling. I like to serve the roasted cod on the Belgian Endive, Tomato, and Melon Salad on page 44. The combination of spicy and sweet is just heavenly.

SERVES 4

- 4 thick pieces of cod fillet (weighing about 6 oz each) skinned
- 2 hot red chiles, deseeded and chopped fine
- 2 garlic cloves, crushed
- 2 Tbsp chopped pitted black olives
- 4 Tbsp thick pumpkin purée, fresh or canned
- Salt and ground black pepper
- 3 Tbsp peanut oil
- 1 tsp butter

Preparation: 10 minutes
Cooking time: 12–15 minutes

❶ Preheat a 425°F oven if you are intending to roast the cod. You could pan-fry the fish if you prefer, but roasting is easier.

❷ Prepare the cod fillets. Make a deep slit with a sharp knife along the top of each fillet—not quite to the ends—to make a pocket for stuffing. Mix together the chiles, garlic, olives, and pumpkin, then season well with salt and pepper. Divide the mixture among the prepared fillets.

❸ Heat the oil with the butter in a large frying pan and brown the cod quickly on both sides. Reduce the heat and continue to cook the cod for 4 to 5 minutes on each side, or transfer it to a buttered baking sheet and roast, stuffing side up, for 6 to 8 minutes. Serve immediately.

fish dishes

59

Broiled Sardines with Spaghetti Squash

Really fresh sardines have a delicious flavor which doesn't want to be challenged by anything else. I have chosen a spaghetti squash to serve with them, but have diced it finely, and added chopped tomato and olives, along with a little olive oil—simple and delicious—rather than boiling it and scooping into strands. Pan-fry the sardines if you prefer, but broiling or barbecuing is best.

SERVES 4

- 1 small spaghetti squash (weighing about 1 lb 10 oz), peeled, deseeded, and diced
- 2 Tbsp extra virgin olive oil
- 1 tsp butter
- 12 fresh sardines, scaled
- 2 large tomatoes, deseeded and diced
- 12 black olives, pitted and diced
- Salt and ground black pepper
- Green salad, to serve

Preparation: 10 minutes
Cooking time: 10 minutes
---

❶ Preheat the broiler. Cook the diced squash in the oil and butter for 3 to 4 minutes, stirring frequently, while broiling the sardines for 2 to 3 minutes on each side. Brush the fish with a little oil before cooking, just to stop them sticking to the broiler rack or pan.

❷ Toss the tomatoes and olives into the pan with the squash and just heat through. Season well, then pile the squash mixture onto warmed serving plates. Add the broiled sardines, a little green salad, and serve immediately.

Hot Chili Haddock with Spaghetti Squash

Spaghetti squash makes an unusual, slightly sweet garnish as it comes away in strands and deep-fries well. For best results, leave the parboiled squash for several hours to dry, so that the strands separate and do not stick together in the hot fat. I like to serve it with battered haddock which is spicily seasoned with a strong chili sauce.

SERVES 3

• ½ small spaghetti squash
• 1 lb 2 oz piece thick haddock fillet, skinned and cut into thirds
• 2 Tbsp seasoned flour

FOR THE HOT CHILI BATTER

• 1 cup flour
• 2 tsp hot chili sauce
• 3 Tbsp sunflower or peanut oil
• 1 cup dark beer
• 1 egg white
• Sunflower oil, for deep-frying
• Lemon wedges, to serve

**Preparation: 20 minutes
+ up to 4 hours drying time
Cooking time: 10 minutes**
---

❶ Cut the squash in half lengthwise and scoop out the seeds. Bring one half to a boil in a pan of salted water, then simmer for 5 minutes. Drain upside-down and leave until cool enough to handle.

❷ Holding the shell upside-down over a baking sheet lined with paper towels, tease out the flesh using a fork. It will come out in strands like spaghetti. Let it fall loosely onto the baking sheet, then leave in a warm kitchen for about 4 hours to dry, or dry in a 300°F oven for 1½ to 2 hours, checking the squash regularly.

❸ Meanwhile, prepare the batter. Beat the flour, chili sauce, oil, and beer together until smooth. Let stand until required.

❹ Heat the oil to 355°F. Beat the egg white until stiff, then fold into the batter just before cooking the fish. Dip the prepared fish in the batter, then gently drop into the oil. Fry for 5 minutes, or until the batter is golden brown and crisp. Drain on plenty of crumpled paper towels. Sprinkle the squash with the seasoned flour, then drop it carefully, a little at a time, into the oil. Fry for just a few seconds until crisp, then remove from the pan with a slotted spoon, and drain well.

❺ Serve the fish, garnished with the deep-fried squash, and lemon wedges, for squeezing over.

fish dishes

Pumpkin Plaice with Zucchini Sauce

I love plaice at lunch time—it is light, summery and not too filling. Mixed with pumpkin it becomes the perfect dish for early fall eating— a little more substantial and comforting, but unlikely to send you off to sleep.

SERVES 2

- 2 plaice fillets (weighing about 6 oz each)
- Salt and white pepper
- 1 Tbsp peanut oil
- 1 tsp butter
- ¾ cup diced, cooked pumpkin
- 2 Tbsp fresh whole wheat bread crumbs
- 2 Tbsp shredded cheese, such as mozzarella or Monterey Jack cheese
- 3 scallions, sliced
- 1 zucchini, sliced fine
- ½ cup light cream
- 2 Tbsp chopped fresh parsley

Preparation: 10 minutes
Cooking time: 12 minutes

❶ Preheat a 425°F oven. Season the plaice fillets lightly on both sides. Heat the oil and butter together in a large frying pan, then add the fillets, skin side up, and brown quickly. Transfer the fillets carefully to a buttered baking sheet.

❷ Mix together the pumpkin, bread crumbs, and cheese. Top the plaice fillets with the pumpkin mixture.

❸ Bake in the oven for 4 to 5 minutes or broil for the same amount of time, until the cheese is melting, the topping has set, and the fish is just cooked.

❹ Add a little more oil to the frying pan if necessary, then stir in the scallions and zucchini, and cook for 3 to 4 minutes, until well softened.

❺ Add the cream and heat until almost bubbling. Blend the sauce until smooth—this is easiest to do with a hand-held blender, but transfer the sauce to a blender or food processor if you wish. Season to taste, then serve the sauce spooned over the fish fillets, garnished with the chopped parsley.

fish dishes

Mixed Fish Cakes with Zucchini Salad

These fish cakes are really light and delicious, and balance a raw vegetable salad very well. Use young, sweet zucchini, and if they are very small add an extra one to the mix.

SERVES 4

- 1 carrot, cut into thin sticks
- 2 zucchini, cut into thin sticks
- 4 scallions, chopped fine
- 2 fresh tomatoes, deseeded and chopped
- 1 mild chile, chopped fine
- 2 Tbsp fish sauce
- 1 Tbsp light soy sauce
- Juice of 1 lemon

FOR THE FISH CAKES

- 2 cups fresh bread crumbs, white or whole wheat
- Milk
- 4 large scallions, sliced fine
- 1 Tbsp peanut oil
- 9 oz salmon fillet, skinned and diced
- 9 oz hoki fillet, skinned and diced
- ⅔ cup shredded zucchini
- Salt and ground black pepper
- 2–3 Tbsp mayonnaise

FOR THE COATING

- ½ cup ground almonds
- 1 cup fresh bread crumbs, white or whole wheat
- ½–1 Tbsp peanut oil, for frying

Preparation: 30–40 minutes
Cooking time: 10 minutes

❶ Combine all the salad ingredients, and leave to stand while preparing the fish cakes.

❷ For the fish cakes, soak the bread crumbs in a little milk for a few minutes, then squeeze dry, and discard the milk. Cook the scallions in the oil in a large frying pan until soft but not browned. Mix with the bread crumbs in a large bowl.

❸ Mix the diced fish with the bread crumbs and all the remaining fish cake ingredients, adding just enough mayonnaise to bind the mixture.

❹ For the coating, mix the bread crumbs and almonds together. Shape the fish mixture into 8 large fish cakes, coating them in the almond crumbs. Press the crumbs into the cakes.

❺ Heat some peanut oil in the frying pan, then add the fish cakes and fry them gently for 4 to 5 minutes on each side. Serve the fish cakes on a bed of the zucchini salad with some of the salad juices.

TIP
Ideally, use one green and one yellow zucchini for the salad.

Fisherman's Pumpkin Pie

Use a selection of fish for this pie, but avoid smoked fillets which would dominate the dish. Keep it uncomplicated, and enjoy the flavors of the simple ingredients. Add a few shelled shrimp if you wish.

SERVES 4

- 4 scallions, sliced fine
- 3 Tbsp peanut oil
- 2½ cups peeled, seeded, and diced pumpkin
- 1 lb 9 oz mixed white fish fillets, skinned and cut into ½-in pieces
- ⅔ cup sour cream
- Salt and white pepper
- 2 Tbsp chopped fresh parsley
- 10–12 sheets filo pastry
- ½ stick butter, melted

Preparation: 20 minutes
Cooking time: 40 minutes

❶ Preheat a 375°F oven. Lightly butter a deep, 8-inch sandwich pan.

❷ Cook the scallions in the oil in a large frying pan for about 2 to 3 minutes—do not let them brown—then add the pumpkin and cook gently for 4 to 5 minutes more, until the squash is just starting to soften. Take the pan off the heat, then stir in the fish, sour cream, and some seasoning with the chopped parsley. Set the filling aside.

❸ Arrange six or seven sheets of filo pastry in the base of the cake pan, draping them over the sides. Brush each sheet with butter, as you use it, to keep it moist and pliable. Pile the filling into the lined pan, then cover it with the remaining sheets of pastry, brushing them with butter as you go.

❹ Roll the edges of the pastry together, then fold them into the pan over the lid of the pie. Brush with any remaining butter and score the pastry lid deeply with a sharp serrated knife into diamonds.

❺ Bake for 30 to 40 minutes, until the pastry is crisp and golden brown. Serve immediately, with a green salad, if you wish.

TIP
When working with filo pastry, place it under a damp dish towel and only take the sheets out as you need them. This prevents them from becoming brittle.

Mussels and Squash with Tomato Spaghetti

Pasta has always been associated with shellfish—shrimp, mussels, clams, and cockles all go well with the thinner, flatter shapes such as spaghetti and tagliatelle. Add some squash and the fish goes further, making a more economical dish.

SERVES 4

- 12 oz dried spaghetti
- 1 large onion, chopped fine
- 3 Tbsp extra virgin olive oil
- 1¾ cups peeled, seeded, and diced butternut squash
- 1 garlic clove, crushed
- 14-oz can chopped tomatoes
- Salt and ground black pepper
- 1½ cups shelled mussels
- 10–12 torn fresh basil leaves

Preparation: 10 minutes
Cooking time: 20 minutes

❶ Bring a very large pan of salted water to a boil, then add the spaghetti, and cook for 15 minutes, or according to the instructions on the package.

❷ While the water is coming to a boil, cook the onion in the oil for 3 to 4 minutes in a large frying pan, until softened but not browned, then add the squash, and cook for 2 to 3 minutes more. Stir in the garlic and tomatoes, with some salt and pepper, then simmer the sauce for 10 minutes, until slightly thickened. Stir in the mussels and cook for 2 to 3 minutes, until piping hot. Season well and add the basil.

❸ Drain the spaghetti and shake it briefly until dry. Add it to the frying pan (or pour the sauce over the spaghetti in the pasta pan if your frying pan isn't big enough) and toss the sauce and pasta together. Mound on to warmed plates and serve immediately.

Squash and Zucchini Trout

Trout are such versatile fish and yet they are so often just served with almonds and slightly burnt butter. A mixture of squash and zucchini complements the oily fish well, and I finish the dish with a fruity orange sauce.

SERVES 4

- 3 Tbsp butter, plus extra
- 1 Tbsp olive oil, plus extra
- 1 zucchini, diced fine
- 1½ cups diced, cooked squash, such as crown prince
- 4 rainbow or brown trout, about 9–10 oz each
- Grated rind and juice of 2 oranges
- 3 kaffir lime leaves, sliced fine
- 1–2 Tbsp plain yogurt
- Salt and ground black pepper

Preparation: 15 minutes
Cooking time: 25 minutes

❶ Heat the butter and oil together in a large frying pan, then add the diced zucchini and squash. Cook for 3 to 4 minutes, until lightly browned, then scoop the vegetables out of the pan into an ovenproof dish, and keep warm.

❷ Add a little extra butter and oil to the pan, then add the trout and fry gently for 5 to 6 minutes on each side. You might have to cook just two at a time. Transfer them to a plate and keep warm in a very low oven while finishing the sauce.

❸ Return the zucchini and squash to the pan with the orange juice and sliced lime leaves. Cook for 1 to 2 minutes, then add the yogurt.

❹ Cook gently until the yogurt has heated through, add the orange rind, and season. Serve the sauce spooned over the fish.

fish dishes

67

Broiled Mackerel with Apple and Cucumber Salsa

Mackerel is a very underrated fish. It is a rich source of the cholesterol-busting omega-3 oils, and is well partnered by a spicy apple and cucumber salsa.

SERVES 4

FOR THE SALSA

- 1 Tbsp white mustard seeds
- 2 tart red eating apples, cored and diced
- ½ medium cucumber, diced
- Grated rind and juice of 1 lemon
- 1 carrot, diced
- 1 hot red chile, deseeded and chopped fine
- 2 fresh tomatoes, deseeded and diced
- 1 Tbsp white wine vinegar
- Salt and ground black pepper

- 8 fresh mackerel fillets
- 1 Tbsp rolled oats

Preparation: 45 minutes

Cooking time: 10 minutes

---

❶ Heat a frying pan, then add the mustard seeds, and fry them for less than 1 minute, until really fragrant. Turn into a bowl, and add all the ingredients for the salsa. Leave for 20 to 30 minutes, to allow the flavors to blend.

❷ Preheat the broiler. Cover the broiler pan rack with lightly oiled foil to make cooking and cleaning up easier. Season the mackerel fillets lightly, then broil skin side up for 3 to 4 minutes, depending on size. Turn the fillets carefully, and broil for a further 3 to 4 minutes, until almost cooked.

❸ Scatter the oats over the fish and cook for 1 to 2 minutes more, until lightly browned.

❹ Serve the mackerel with plenty of salsa, and some freshly boiled potatoes, tossed in butter and chopped parsley, if you wish.

TIP

The apples, cucumber, carrot, and tomatoes should be cut into even-size dice—about ¼ inch thick.

fish dishes

Scallops with Baby Patty Pans and Bacon

I have always enjoyed scallops cooked with bacon—the two flavors are very complementary. I have chosen to include a recipe for this winning combination that is quick, easy, and comes with its own sauce.

Serves 3–4

- 9 oz baby patty pan squash, topped, tailed, and halved horizontally
- 6 slices bacon, rinded and chopped
- 2 Tbsp extra virgin olive oil
- 1 lb scallops, sliced horizontally
- 2 garlic cloves, sliced fine
- 6 scallions, sliced fine
- ⅔ cup dry white wine
- ⅔ cup light cream
- Salt and white pepper
- 1–2 Tbsp freshly chopped parsley
- 8-10 oz black spaghetti
- Paprika, to garnish

Preparation: 10 minutes

Cooking time: 25 minutes

❶ Cook the squash and bacon in the oil over medium heat until the squash are just starting to soften—about 3 minutes—stirring frequently.

❷ Add the scallops and cook quickly for 30 to 60 seconds on each side, until they are a bold white color, then add the garlic, scallions, and wine. Bring to a boil, scraping up any bits from the base of the pan, add the cream, and season.

❸ Continue cooking briefly, for just 1 to 2 minutes, until all the ingredients are piping hot. Stir in the chopped parsley.

❹ To serve: drain the cooked black spaghetti and mold into nests in the center of warmed serving plates. Spoon the scallops and squash into the nests then spoon the sauce over. Sprinkle with paprika and serve immediately.

fish dishes

69

Squid and Pumpkin Stew with Tomatoes

So many people are put off squid when they have it badly fried and chewy. It should either be cooked very briefly, or stewed for a long time. This serves as a soup or main meal.

SERVES 4

- 1 large onion, chopped fine
- 3 Tbsp extra virgin olive oil
- 3 cups peeled, seeded, and diced pumpkin
- 1 lb prepared squid rings
- 2 garlic cloves, sliced fine
- 2 tsp paprika
- 2 cups puréed tomatoes or thick tomato juice
- 1 cup fish or vegetable stock
- 2 bay leaves
- Salt and ground black pepper
- light cream and chopped fresh parsley, to garnish

Preparation: 20 minutes
Cooking time: 2 hours

❶ Cook the onion for 5 to 6 minutes in the oil in a large pan over low heat, until softened but not browned. Add the pumpkin, continue to cook for 3 to 4 minutes, then stir in the squid. Increase the heat and cook for 2 to 3 minutes, until the squid is opaque, then add the garlic and paprika. Lower the heat and continue cooking for a further 2 to 3 minutes.

❷ Add the puréed tomatoes or tomato juice, the stock, and bay leaves. Season well, then bring the stew slowly to a boil. Cover, and cook over very low heat for 1½–2 hours, stirring occasionally.

❸ Remove the bay leaves, then adjust the seasoning if necessary. Add a little water if the stew has become too thick.

❹ Serve in warmed bowls with a swirl of cream and a scattering of freshly chopped parsley.

Lamb and Pumpkin Moussaka

Mexican Chili with Spicy Squash

Spiced Lamb with Pumpkin and Garbanzo Beans

Roasted Lamb with Butternut Squash

Beef, Squash, and Mustard Pie

Spiced Beef and Squash Stew with Couscous

Rich Daube of Beef with Baby Patty Pan Squash

Roasted Sausage and Squash with Red Cabbage

Kabocha and Celery Stuffed Ham Rolls

Normandy Pork Fillet with Apples and Squash

Pot-roasted Pork with Squash

"Confit" of Duck with Gingered Pumpkin

Baked Onion Squash with Mexican Chicken

Brown Rice Chicken Paella

Pumpkin Pizza with Chicken

Chicken and Zucchini Sauce for Pasta

Turkey, Pumpkin, and Cranberry Pie

Turkey and Squash Fricassée

Lamb and Pumpkin Moussaka

Moussaka is traditionally made with eggplant, but it is actually rather good, for a change, with sliced pumpkin or squash. Try it—it's refreshingly different.

SERVES 6

- 1 large onion, chopped fine
- 2 Tbsp olive oil
- 1 lb 2 oz ground lamb
- 14-oz can chopped tomatoes
- 1 Tbsp tomato paste
- 1 garlic clove, crushed
- Salt and ground black pepper
- Freshly grated nutmeg
- 1 Tbsp chopped fresh oregano or marjoram
- 10–12 x ¼-in slices pumpkin or squash, peeled and deseeded

FOR THE TOPPING

- 1 cup plain yogurt
- 1 cup sour cream
- ⅔ cup soft goat cheese, plain or with garlic and herbs

Preparation: 45 minutes
Cooking time: 50 minutes

---

❶ Cook the onion in the oil until soft but not browned, then add the ground lamb, and cook over slightly higher heat until there is no pink meat left. Stir frequently to break up any lumps that form in the pan. Add all the remaining sauce ingredients, then bring to a boil. Simmer slowly for 30 minutes.

❷ Preheat a 375°F oven. The number of pumpkin or squash slices you will require will depend on the variety used. Layer the meat with the pumpkin or squash in a suitable buttered ovenproof dish, finishing with a layer of pumpkin or squash.

❸ Beat the yogurt, sour cream, and goat cheese together with some salt and pepper. Spread the mixture over the top of the moussaka. Place the dish on a baking sheet and cook in the oven for 45 to 50 minutes, or until the topping is browned and the squash is tender enough when a skewer is inserted into the center of the dish.

❹ Let stand for a few minutes before serving with a tomato salad and fresh green leaves, or green vegetables, if you wish.

Mexican Chili with Spicy Squash

Pan-fried, spicy, starchy squash is added to this chili at the end of cooking instead of pinto or red kidney beans. The result is sweeter than the average chili—and much more interesting.

SERVES 4

- 2 onions, chopped
- 2 tsp chili powder, or to taste
- 1 tsp ground cumin
- 6 Tbsp peanut oil
- 1 lb 2 oz ground lamb
- 1 Tbsp chopped fresh oregano
- 1 large cinnamon stick
- 2 garlic cloves, crushed
- 1–2 mild green chiles, deseeded and chopped (optional)
- 14-oz can chopped tomatoes
- 1 Tbsp tomato paste
- Salt and ground black pepper
- 4 cups peeled, seeded, and diced squash, such as kabocha or crown prince
- 1 tsp cumin seeds
- Sour cream and snipped fresh chives, to serve

Preparation: 10 minutes

Cooking time: 1½ hours or more

❶ Cook the onion with the chili powder and ground cumin in half the oil over low heat for 4 to 5 minutes, until the onions are soft. Add the lamb, increase the heat slightly, and cook until the lamb is well browned, then add the oregano, cinnamon, and garlic. Add the chiles, if using, with the chopped tomatoes, tomato paste, and seasoning, and stir well.

❷ Bring the chili to a boil, then cover the pan, and simmer slowly for at least 1 hour.

❸ Fry the squash in the remaining oil for 4 to 5 minutes, until browned and just soft, then add the cumin seeds, and cook for 1 minute more. Add the squash to the chili, then season again. Serve topped with a dollop of sour cream with fresh snipped chives scattered over. You could provide tortilla chips or garlic bread as an accompaniment.

meat and poultry

Spiced Lamb with Pumpkin and Garbanzo Beans

Heavy with Middle Eastern flavors, this spicy lamb stew can be made with either pumpkin or squash, but I think pumpkin works best as it is not quite so starchy with the garbanzo beans. Serve with some sautéed potatoes and a tomato or green salad, or perhaps some green beans or zucchini.

SERVES 4

- ½ cup dried garbanzo beans, soaked overnight
- 3 Tbsp olive oil, plus extra
- 8 oz lamb neck fillet, sliced
- 1 onion, sliced fine
- 4 cups peeled, seeded, and diced pumpkin
- 2 tsp ground cumin
- 1 tsp ground allspice
- 1 cinnamon stick, broken
- ⅔ cup red wine
- 14-oz can chopped tomatoes
- 1½ cups well-flavored stock
- ½ cup ready-to-eat dried apricots
- Salt and ground black pepper
- ⅓ cup pistachios
- Chopped fresh cilantro, to garnish

Preparation: 45 minutes and overnight soaking

Cooking time: 1 hour

---

❶ Drain the garbanzo beans and rinse thoroughly under cold running water. Bring to a boil in a pan of fresh water, then cover, and simmer for 30 to 40 minutes.

❷ Fry the lamb in the oil until browned on all sides, then remove from the pan with a slotted spoon, and set aside. Add the onion to the pan, cook over medium-high heat until lightly browned, then add the pumpkin and a little extra oil if necessary. Cook for 2 to 3 minutes, then stir in the spices, and continue cooking over low heat for another 1 to 2 minutes.

❸ Return the lamb fillet to the pan and add the wine. Bring to a boil, stirring all the time to scrape up any tasty bits from the base of the pan, then simmer until reduced by at least half. Stir in the tomatoes, stock, and apricots, and add a little seasoning. Drain the garbanzo beans, add them to the stew, cover, and simmer for 30 minutes.

❹ Add the pistachios to the lamb and season to taste, removing the cinnamon stick. Serve garnished with chopped fresh cilantro.

Roasted Lamb with Butternut Squash

This is so simple, it's not really a recipe at all, but too delicious a combination of flavors to leave out of this book.

SERVES 6

- 1 leg of lamb (weighing 3 lb 5 oz–3 lb 13 oz)
- 2 garlic cloves
- Salt and ground black pepper
- 1 butternut squash, quartered and deseeded

Preparation: 5 minutes

Cooking time: about 2 hours

---

❶ Everyone has their favorite method of roasting lamb, so you can cook this quickly or slowly, whichever you prefer. Remember the squash will need about 45 minutes in a hot oven or around 1 hour at a more moderate temperature. Always allow 20 minutes for the joint to stand before carving, and build this into your schedule.

❷ Preheat a 400°F oven. Place the lamb in a roasting pan. Make some deep slits in the lamb and fill them with slivers of garlic. Calculate the roasting time by allowing 55 minutes per 2 lb 4 oz—just under 2 hours for this size leg of lamb. Season and roast for 1¼ hours.

❸ Add the squash to the roasting pan and baste with the meat juices. Roast for 30 minutes, remove the

lamb, and wrap in foil. Continue roasting the squash until tender.

❹ Carve the lamb, and serve the slices with the squash, and vegetables of your choice.

TIP

Instead of using slivers of garlic to stud the lamb, try sprigs of rosemary or pieces of anchovy instead.

---

meat and poultry

Beef, Squash, and Mustard Pie

My Mom's steak and kidney pie was always one of my favorite dishes as a child. I have long since given up trying to make that particular dish as well as she does, but this pie which teams the beef with a firm winter squash is a good alternative. You could simmer the beef slowly on the stove if you prefer.

SERVES 6

- 1 large onion, sliced fine
- 2 Tbsp oil
- 1 lb 2 oz chuck steak, trimmed and cut into bite-size pieces
- 2 Tbsp dark soy sauce
- 2 star anise
- Ground black pepper
- 2 cups light beer, plus extra if needed
- 4 x 1-in slices (12 oz) crown prince squash
- 2 Tbsp whole grain mustard
- 8 oz ready-made puff pastry

Preparation: 30 minutes

Cooking time: 4 hours and 40 minutes

❶ Preheat a 325°F oven. Cook the onion in the oil over medium-high heat until just starting to brown, then add the beef, and continue cooking until both are well browned on all sides. Transfer the meat to a casserole or pie dish, add the soy sauce, and bury the star anise in the meat. Season well with pepper.

❷ Add the beer to the pan and bring to a boil, stirring all the time to scrape up any sediment. Pour the beer over the meat, adding a little extra as necessary just to cover the meat. Cover the casserole and cook in the oven for 2½–3 hours, or until the beef is tender. Allow to cool.

❸ Reheat the oven to 425°F. Place the squash in a roasting pan, then season lightly, and drizzle with oil. Roast the squash for 40 minutes, or until tender. Leave to cool for 10 to 15 minutes. Lower the oven temperature to 400°F.

❹ Trim away the skin from the squash and chop the flesh into 1-inch dice. Stir the squash into the beef with the mustard.

❺ Roll out the pastry and use to cover the beef and squash. Use any trimmings to decorate the pie, then bake for 35 to 40 minutes, until the pastry is golden brown.

TIP

I often cook the meat in advance and leave it to cool completely before covering with the pastry.

meat and poultry

76

Spiced Beef and Squash Stew with Couscous

Flavored with cumin and chili, two widely used spices in northern Africa, this stew is served with a mound of couscous in the middle of each helping in large, dished plates. It makes a satisfying meal.

Serves 4

- 3 Tbsp olive oil
- 1 lb 2 oz chuck steak, cut into 1-in pieces
- 1 large onion, sliced fine
- 2 tsp mild chili powder
- 2 tsp ground cumin
- 1 large cinnamon stick
- 1–2 hot red chiles, deseeded and chopped fine
- 1 lb 9 oz peeled, seeded winter squash, cut into 1-in pieces
- ⅔ cup red wine
- 2 zucchini, diced
- 2 garlic cloves
- 14-oz can chopped tomatoes
- 2½ cups well-flavored stock
- Salt and ground black pepper
- 1 cup couscous

Preparation: 30 minutes

Cooking time: 2½ hours

---

❶ Preheat a 325°F oven. Heat the oil in a flameproof casserole, brown the beef, then remove it from the pan with a slotted spoon.

❷ Add the onion to the casserole, cook quickly until well browned but not burnt, then add the spices and chiles with the squash. Continue to cook over low heat for 6 to 8 minutes, until the squash softens.

❸ Return the beef to the pan with the red wine and bring slowly to a boil, stirring all the time to scrape up any sediment from the base of the pan. Add the diced zucchini with the garlic, then the chopped tomatoes, and sufficient stock to just cover the meat, about 1½ cups. Season well then bring the stew slowly to a boil. Cover, transfer to the oven, and cook for 2 to 2½ hours.

❹ Just before the beef is ready, bring the remaining stock to a boil in a saucepan. Add the couscous, then cover, and leave, off the heat, for about 10 minutes, until the grains have absorbed the liquid and become fluffy. Moisten with a little olive oil if necessary, then serve with the beef.

TIP

You could serve this dish simply on a bed of green vegetables.

---

meat and poultry

Rich Daube of Beef with Baby Patty Pan Squash

A daube is a rich beef stew from the Burgundy region of France, traditionally seasoned with orange.

SERVES 6

- 2 lb chuck steak, cut into 2-in pieces
- 3 Tbsp extra virgin olive oil
- 1 large onion, sliced
- 8 oz bacon, chopped
- 2 large carrots, sliced thick
- 1 Tbsp red wine vinegar
- 3 large sprigs fresh thyme
- 1 large cinnamon stick, broken
- 4 bay leaves
- ½ tsp cloves
- 2–3 garlic cloves, sliced fine
- Grated rind of 1 large orange
- 1 bottle red wine
- 2 Tbsp tomato paste
- Salt and ground black pepper
- 1 lb 2 oz baby patty pan squash, topped and tailed
- 2 Tbsp chopped fresh parsley

Preparation: 20–25 minutes
Cooking time: 3¼ hours

❶ Preheat a 325°F oven. Cook the beef in the oil in a large flameproof skillet over medium-high heat until well browned on both sides.

❷ Remove the beef from the pan and add the onion, bacon, and carrots. Cook over low heat until the onions are tender and starting to brown. Add the vinegar and stir until all the sediment from the base of the pan has been scraped up.

❸ Return the beef to the pan, then add all the herbs and spices, garlic, orange rind, wine, and tomato paste with some seasoning. Bring slowly to a boil, then cover the pan, and transfer to the oven. Cook for 3 hours, or until the beef is tender.

❹ Trim the patty pans. Season the daube to taste, removing the bay leaves, cinnamon, and twigs from the thyme, then add the squash. Cover and cook in the oven for 10 to 15 minutes more, or until the squash are just tender. Garnish with parsley, then serve with your choice of potatoes, rice, or pasta.

Roasted Sausage and Squash with Red Cabbage

I have always loved sausages, especially high-quality, coarse-cut, prime meat varieties. The squash sweetens the cabbage well, and makes the sausages go further.

SERVES 4

- 8 thick sausages, pork, beef or venison
- 4 x 1-in slices (12 oz) winter squash, such as Hubbard, crown prince, or kabocha
- Salt and ground black pepper

FOR THE CABBAGE

- 1 large onion, chopped fine
- 1 Tbsp mustard seeds
- 3 Tbsp olive oil
- 2 cups sliced red cabbage
- 1 Tbsp red wine vinegar
- ½ cup red wine
- Salt and ground black pepper

Preparation: 10 minutes

Cooking time: 45 minutes

❶ Preheat a 400°F oven. Arrange the sausages and the squash in a roasting pan. Season the squash, then cook in the oven for 40 to 45 minutes, until the squash is tender.

❷ Cook the onion and the mustard seeds in the oil for 2 minutes, then add the cabbage, and continue to cook for 2 minutes more. Stir in the vinegar and wine and seasonings, then cover the pan and simmer the cabbage for 30 minutes.

❸ Cut away the skin from the squash, then dice the flesh, and stir it into the cabbage. Season to taste, then serve with the sausages.

TIP

Unless your sausages have natural skins, remember to prick them with a fork before cooking them in the oven, to prevent them from splitting.

Kabocha and Celery Stuffed Ham Rolls

An unusual Thai-flavored sweet-and-sour filling for creamy baked ham rolls. These would make a good appetizer before a light main course but also make an excellent lunch or supper dish.

SERVES 4

- 3 Tbsp peanut oil
- 1 onion, sliced fine
- 3 cups peeled, seeded, and diced kabocha squash
- 1 stalk lemon grass, bruised and chopped fine
- 2 cups chopped celery
- 1 red chile, deseeded and chopped fine (optional)
- 1 tsp tamarind paste
- 4 large slices of ham
- 2 kaffir lime leaves, sliced fine
- 1¼ cups light cream
- Salt and ground black pepper

Preparation: 30 minutes

Cooking time: 20 minutes

❶ Heat the oil in a large frying pan, add the onion, and cook until just starting to brown—do this over medium–high heat so that the onion softens as well.

❷ Add the squash with the lemon grass and celery, and continue to cook for 4 to 5 minutes before adding the chile and tamarind paste. Stir well, then continue to cook slowly for about 15 minutes, until the squash is almost tender.

❸ Meanwhile, preheat a 375°F oven and lightly butter a suitable gratin dish. Divide the squash filling among the four slices of ham and roll up carefully. Spoon any leftover filling into the base of the dish, then arrange the ham rolls on top. Stir the lime leaves into the cream, adding just a little seasoning, then pour over the rolls into the dish.

❹ Bake for 20 minutes, until the cream is lightly browned. Serve immediately, with stir-fried vegetables and rice, if you wish.

TIP

Instead of cream, use coconut milk for the sauce. Or you could use a combination of the two.

Normandy Pork Fillet with Apples and Squash

This dish is based on the many traditional Normandy dishes of chicken or pheasant cooked with apples and calvados, the apple brandy of northern France.

SERVES 3–4

- 2 Tbsp olive oil, plus extra
- 1 tsp butter
- 1 gem squash, peeled, deseeded, and sliced
- 1 sharp green eating apple, cored and sliced
- 1 lb 2 oz pork fillet, trimmed and cut into ½-in slices
- 1 onion, sliced finely
- 1 garlic clove, chopped fine
- 1 cup hard cider
- Salt and ground black pepper
- ⅔ cup calvados or brandy
- 2–3 Tbsp sour cream
- Chopped fresh parsley, to garnish

Preparation: 10 minutes

Cooking time: 30 minutes

❶ Heat the oil and butter together in a large frying pan, then cook the squash until softened and browned on both sides. Remove with a slotted spoon, then repeat with the apple rings. Set aside with the squash.

❷ Add extra oil if necessary, then add the sliced pork, and cook in the same way. Stir in the onion and cook until starting to brown. Add the garlic, cider, and season. Bring to a boil, stirring to scrape up any sediment from the base of the pan, then simmer slowly for 15 minutes.

❸ Heat the calvados or brandy slowly until it ignites. Pour into the pork, off the heat. Leave until the flames subside.

❹ Stir the sour cream into the pan with the squash and apple, and heat gently until the cream has combined with the sauce, and the squash and apples are hot. Season to taste, then serve garnished with the chopped fresh parsley.

Pot-roasted Pork with Squash

I have long enjoyed meat or poultry with fruit juices. Chicken and peaches is a favorite and somehow this very fragrant sauce with pot-roasted pork reminds me of it.

SERVES 6

- 1 joint sparerib of pork (weighing about 3 lb 5 oz)
- 2 Tbsp peanut oil
- 1 large onion, sliced fine
- 2 carrots, chopped
- 4 celery stalks, chopped
- 1 lb 2 oz peeled, seeded winter squash, such as crown prince or kabocha, chopped
- 1 garlic clove, crushed
- 1 Tbsp chopped arugula, or 3 Tbsp chopped fresh parsley
- 2–3 blades mace
- Salt and ground black pepper
- 1¼ cups well-flavored vegetable or chicken stock

Preparation: 15–20 minutes

Cooking time: 2½ hours

❶ Preheat a 325°F oven. Brown the pork in the oil in a heavy flameproof casserole over high heat. Remove from the pan.

❷ Add all the prepared vegetables, except the garlic, and toss in the oily juices. Cook over medium heat until they begin to soften and brown. Add the garlic, lovage or parsley, and the mace, then arrange the meat in the pan on the vegetables.

❸ Pour the stock into the pan and bring slowly to a boil. Cover, then cook in the oven for at least 2 hours, preferably 2½ hours, until the pork is tender. Lift the meat from the pan, wrap in foil, and leave to rest for 15 minutes before carving. If you wish, you could cut the crackling off the joint at this stage and cook it under the grill until crispy. Chopped up, it makes a contrasting garnish.

❹ Blend the vegetables and pan juices to a thick sauce and season well. Use a hand-held blender or blend in a blender or food processor. Carve the pork, and serve it with the sauce spooned over.

meat and poultry

"Confit" of Duck with Gingered Pumpkin

I love confit but I have always felt that it must take ages to prepare, and be a very sticky, greasy job to accomplish. Well, this quick way of doing it may not be wholly authentic, but it is very rich, delicious, and easy. It is also a good dish for entertaining, as the duckling benefits from being cooked a day in advance. I use pumpkin rather than squash as it is softer and blends into the noodles more easily.

SERVES 4
- 4 duckling leg portions
- Chicken fat
- ⅔ cup water
- Peanut oil
- 4 x 1-in slices (12 oz) of pumpkin, deseeded

FOR THE MARINADE
- 3 Tbsp chopped fresh ginger root
- 2 large garlic cloves, crushed
- 1 Tbsp star anise
- 1 tsp ground white pepper
- 2 Tbsp coarse sea salt

- 2 oz dried thread egg noodles
- 8 scallions, sliced diagonally
- 1 Tbsp white wine vinegar
- 2-in piece fresh ginger root, chopped
- Fresh cilantro, to garnish

Preparation: 1 hour,
plus overnight marinating time
Cooking time: 1½ hours plus 1 hour

❶ Trim the duckling legs, removing any excess skin. Scrape any fat from the skin and chop roughly. Place the fat in a small pan with any chicken fat that you may have, and the water. Bring to a boil, then cover, and simmer slowly for 45 minutes, or until all the fat is clear.

❷ Marinate the duckling in a dish by scattering the spices evenly over the portions. Use just enough salt to give a good covering to the top surface of the duck, then set aside. Leave to marinate for 1 hour minimum, preferably overnight.

❸ Preheat a 400°F oven. Rinse the duckling portions under cold running water to remove all the salt and spices, then pack into a casserole which will just take them snugly. Strain the fat mixture over the duckling legs, and add sufficient peanut oil to cover the portions completely. Cover the dish and cook in the oven for 30 minutes, then reduce the heat to 325°F, and cook for 1 hour more, or until the duckling is very tender but not falling off the bone. Leave to cool in the fat, preferably overnight.

meat and poultry

❹ When cool or the next day, preheat a 425°F oven. Place the pumpkin in a roasting pan, season lightly, and smear with a little of the fat from the marinated duckling. Cook in the oven for 30 minutes.

❺ Remove the duckling from the fat and scrape off the excess. Place the portions in the roasting pan with the pumpkin and cook for 20 to 25 minutes, turning once. Remove the pumpkin after 10 to 15 minutes, once tender, and turn the duckling. At the same time, strain off and reserve most of the fat. Leave sufficient to keep the meat moist and to prevent it from sticking to the pan.

❻ Meanwhile, cover the noodles with boiling water and let stand for 5 minutes before draining. Measure 2 tablespoons of the drained duck fat into a pan, add the scallions, and cook briefly. Add the vinegar, then squeeze the juice from the ginger shreds into the pan. Fork the pumpkin into strands, scraping it from the skin, and add it to the scallions with the drained noodles. Season to taste.

❼ Make a small pile of pumpkin noodles on each of four warmed serving plates, then place a piece of confit on each. Spoon a little of the fat over, with any juices from the noodles, garnish with cilantro, and serve immediately.

meat and poultry

Baked Onion Squash with Mexican Chicken

Onion squash replaces flour tortillas as the holder for a spicy Mexican chicken filling, served topped with sour cream. This is a filling meal which requires only a small Mexican-style salad of lettuce, scallions, tomato, and avocado to accompany it.

SERVES 2

- 1 small onion squash (weighing about 1 lb 12 oz)
- ¼ stick butter
- 2 garlic cloves, crushed
- 1 hot red chile, deseeded and chopped fine
- 3 Tbsp peanut oil
- 2 chicken breast fillets, skinned and diced
- 1 onion, chopped fine
- 1–2 tsp chili powder
- 1 tsp ground cumin
- 1 green bell pepper, deseeded and sliced
- 1 cup canned chopped tomatoes
- Salt and ground black pepper
- Sour cream, to serve

Preparation: 25 minutes
Cooking time: 30 minutes

---

❶ Preheat a 425°F oven. Top and tail the squash, then cut it in half horizontally. Scoop out the seeds and score the flesh in the two halves deeply before placing them in a small roasting pan or gratin dish. Melt the butter, stir in half the garlic, and the chopped chile, then brush the mixture over the squash, letting it trickle into the score marks. Roast the squash for 15 minutes or so, while preparing the filling.

❷ Heat the oil in a large frying pan, then add the diced chicken, and cook until beginning to brown. Add the onion, remaining garlic, and spices, then reduce the heat, and continue to cook gently for 4 to 5 minutes, until the onion has softened. Stir from time to time to prevent the spices from burning.

❸ Add the bell pepper and tomatoes, and bring the mixture to a boil, stirring all the time to scrape up any sediment from the base of the pan.

❹ Season well, then pile the filling into the half-cooked squash shells. Cover loosely with foil, then return the squash to the oven for 15 minutes.

❺ Remove the foil, then continue to roast the filled squash for 10 to 15 minutes more, until the squash is tender and both the vegetable shells and the filling are starting to blacken. Serve immediately, topped with sour cream.

Pumpkin Pizza with Chicken

This is a really novel pizza with a Mediterranean accent, using wonderfully unusual but complementary ingredients.

SERVES 3–4

- 2½ cups strong white bread flour
- 2 tsp salt
- 1 Tbsp dried yeast
- 3 Tbsp extra virgin olive oil
- 14-oz can pumpkin purée
- About ⅔ cup warm water
- 7 oz mozzarella cheese
- 1 large onion, sliced fine
- 8 oz cooked chicken breast, sliced
- 3 Tbsp small black olives
- 2 Tbsp capers
- Olive oil, for drizzling

Preparation: 1 hour
Cooking time: 25 minutes

❶ Mix the flour with the salt and dried yeast in a bowl, then add the oil, half the pumpkin purée, and sufficient water to mix to a manageable bread dough. Knead thoroughly until smooth and elastic.

❷ Flour a large baking sheet. Roll the dough out to a circle about 15 inches in diameter and lift it on to the baking sheet—it doesn't matter if it overlaps the sides of the baking sheet slightly at this stage.

❸ Shred half the mozzarella and scatter it around the edge of the dough. Damp the crust and fold it over the cheese, leaving a circle about 12 inches in diameter. Cover with a damp cloth and leave the dough to rise for about 40 minutes.

❹ Preheat a 425°F oven. Spread the remaining pumpkin over the risen pizza base, then top with the sliced onion, chicken, olives, and capers. Season well, then top with the remaining mozzarella, thinly sliced, and drizzle with a little olive oil.

❺ Bake for 20 to 25 minutes, until the crust is golden brown. Serve in wedges, with a tossed green salad if you wish.

Chicken and Zucchini Sauce for Pasta

Ground chicken is now widely available in supermarkets. For a dish like this, which has a very rich tomato sauce, poultry is ideal as it is lower in fat than the more traditional beef or lamb.

SERVES 4

- 1 large onion, chopped fine
- 2 Tbsp extra virgin olive oil
- 1 lb 2 oz ground chicken
- ⅔ cup red wine
- 3 zucchini, diced
- 2 garlic cloves, crushed
- 4 halves sun-dried tomatoes in oil, sliced
- 1 cup sliced cup mushrooms
- 14-oz can chopped tomatoes
- 1 Tbsp tomato paste
- 2 Tbsp chopped fresh oregano
- Salt and ground black pepper

Preparation: 10 minutes
Cooking time: Anything from 45 minutes to 1¼–1½ hours, the longer the better

❶ Cook the onion in the oil over low heat until softened but not browned, then add the ground chicken, and cook slightly more quickly, until no pink meat is left. Stir frequently to break up any lumps of meat that may form in the pan. Add the wine, then continue to cook over medium-high heat until reduced by at least one third.

❷ Add the remaining ingredients, and season well with salt and pepper. Bring the sauce to a boil, then simmer slowly for at least 30 minutes—up to 1 hour is ideal.

❸ Season the sauce again before serving. Toss into freshly cooked pasta and sprinkle with Parmesan.

TIP

If you prefer, use ground turkey in this recipe. This resulting dish will be equally good.

Turkey, Pumpkin, and Cranberry Pie

Raised pies are brilliant for busy weekends when you cannot foresee time in the kitchen as they can be baked ahead. This pie is particularly moist—the cranberries cook down juicily, and the turkey and pumpkin are kept succulent by the fatty belly pork.

SERVES 8

FOR THE HOT WATER PASTRY CRUST

- 3 cups flour
- 2 tsp salt
- ½ cup shortening
- ⅔ cup mixed milk and water

FOR THE FILLING

- 1 lb 5 oz boneless turkey breast, diced fine
- 14 oz belly pork, rinded and chopped fine
- 2 cups peeled, seeded, and diced pumpkin
- 1½ cups fresh cranberries
- 2-in piece fresh ginger root, sliced fine and squeezed
- 1 tsp cardamom seeds, crushed
- Freshly grated nutmeg
- Grated rind and juice of 1 orange
- 1 tsp salt
- ½ tsp ground black pepper

- 1 large egg, beaten
- 1 Tbsp gelatin
- 1 cup boiling water

Preparation: 45–50 minutes
Cooking time: 1½ hours

❶ Preheat a 400°F oven. For the pastry, mix the flour and salt in a large bowl and make a well in the center. Melt the shortening into the milk and water in a small pan, bring to a boil, then pour immediately into the flour. Mix to a soft, manageable dough, then turn onto the work surface, and knead lightly until smooth. Cover the pastry with the upturned mixing bowl and let stand until cool enough to handle.

❷ For the filling, mix all the ingredients together, using about half a nutmeg for seasoning.

❸ Roll out two thirds of the pastry into a large circle and use to line a 9-inch, 2-inch deep springform pan. Press the pastry well into the corners and up the side of the pan. Pack in the filling, pressing it down firmly with the back of a spoon, then roll out the remaining pastry into a circular lid for the pie. Brush the edges of the pastry with egg, then press both crusts together, and seal. Use your fingers to press the pastry into a decorative edge. Make a small slit in the center of the lid to allow the steam to escape.

❹ Add a pinch of salt to the beaten egg, and use to brush the lid of the pie. Set aside any remaining egg. Bake for about 1 hour then carefully run a knife between the side of the pan and the pastry. This will loosen the pie from the edge—meat juices may have escaped and made the pastry stick. Open the spring on the pan and remove the side. If the pan will not release the pie without tearing the pastry, return to the oven for 10 to 15 minutes more, then try again. Place the pie on a baking sheet, and brush the sides and top with half the reserved beaten egg. Bake for 30 minutes more, brushing the pie again with egg after 15 minutes.

❺ Let the pie cool. Stir the gelatin or aspic into the hot water, then leave to dissolve completely. Cool slightly, but do not allow the mixture to set. Carefully pour the jelly mixture into the pie, through the slit in the lid, until you can force no more in. Chill the pie for at least 3 hours before slicing and serving.

meat and poultry

Turkey and Squash Fricassée

If you are a real squash enthusiast like me, there will be times when you have a selection of leftovers in the vegetable basket. This is an ideal dish for using them up, along with any leftover turkey.

SERVES 4

- 3 Tbsp oil
- 6 scallions, chopped
- 1 cup diced cooked chicken
- 6 cups peeled, seeded, and diced mixed winter squash
- ½ cup dry white wine
- 1 cup sour cream
- Salt and ground black pepper
- Boiled rice, to serve
- Chopped fresh parsley, to garnish

Preparation: 10–15 minutes
Cooking time: 20 minutes

---

❶ Heat the oil in a large frying pan, add the scallions and chicken, and cook quickly for 2 to 3 minutes, then add the squash. Toss to coat, then cover the pan, and cook slowly for about 10 minutes, until the cubes of squash have softened.

❷ Pour the wine into the pan and cook quickly, stirring all the time, until reduced by half. Stir in the sour cream, season to taste, then heat gently without boiling.

❸ Serve on a bed of rice, garnished with chopped parsley.

TIP

If you wish, add a few mushrooms to this dish but make sure they are closed cup mushrooms so they do not discolor the fricassée.

Acorn Squash with Lentil and Celery Sauce

Spinach and Zucchini Pie

Butternut Squash and Cauliflower Bake

Mediterranean Baked Stuffed Squash

Roasted Pumpkin Ratatouille Cobbler

Curried Banana Squash

Squash Stuffed Roasted Bell Peppers

Pumpkin and Navy Bean Cassoulet

Baked Stuffed Patty Pan Squash

Blue Cheese and Pecan Risotto with Squash

Squash and Okra Curry

Savory Country Pumpkin Pie

Kabocha, Fennel, and Orange Casserole

Squash and Apricot Bulgur Risotto

Spiced Pumpkin Soufflé

Acorn Squash with Lentil and Celery Sauce

A relatively quick dish to cook, but one which is filling and full of flavor. I like to use a ridged grill pan to cook the squash, as the appearance is then so attractive, but an ordinary frying pan will cook it.

SERVES 4

- 1 onion, chopped
- 4 celery stalks, chopped
- 3 Tbsp olive oil, plus extra
- ½ cup lentils
- ½ cup red wine
- 14-oz can chopped tomatoes
- 1–2 cloves garlic, crushed
- 4 large sprigs thyme
- 2 bay leaves
- 1 acorn squash, trimmed
- Salt and ground black pepper

Preparation: 10 minutes

Cooking time: 40 minutes

❶ Cook the onion and celery in the oil until softened but not browned, then add the lentils and wine. Simmer until the wine is slightly reduced, then add the chopped tomatoes, garlic, and herbs. Bring to a boil, then simmer for 30 minutes, until the sauce has thickened and the lentils are tender.

❷ Cut the squash, unpeeled, into four thick rings and remove the seeds. Preheat a griddle pan or a large frying pan, and add a little olive oil. Cook the squash for 5 minutes on each side over medium heat, pressing down firmly at first, to encourage the marking from the griddle if used. The squash rings may be kept warm in a medium oven if necessary.

❸ Season the sauce well with salt and pepper, then remove the thyme and bay leaves. Serve the sauce spooned over the squash rings, with freshly cooked green vegetables.

Spinach and Zucchini Pie

A variation on the popular Greek spinach pie Spanakopitta. *The shredded zucchini give it more body and texture.*

SERVES 6

- 1 large onion, chopped
- 2 Tbsp olive oil
- 3½ cups shredded zucchini
- 4 cups fresh leaf spinach, sliced
- 2 garlic cloves, crushed
- 3 Tbsp pumpkin seeds
- Salt, ground black pepper, and freshly grated nutmeg
- 1 cup cream cheese
- 12–15 sheets filo pastry
- ½ stick butter, melted

Preparation: 25 minutes
Cooking time 30 minutes

❶ Preheat a 400°F oven. Cook the onion in the olive oil until soft, then add the zucchini, and stir-fry for 2 to 3 minutes.

❷ Add the chopped spinach (with just the water clinging to it after washing) with the garlic, and continue to cook over high heat, stirring constantly, for 2 to 3 minutes, until the spinach has wilted and most of the water has evaporated.

❸ Remove the pan from the heat, add the pumpkin seeds, and season well with salt, pepper, and nutmeg.

Stir in the cream cheese, allowing it to melt over the hot vegetables.

❹ Line a deep 8-inch sandwich pan, preferably with a removable base, with sheets of filo pastry, brushed with melted butter, letting them drape over the sides of the pan. The pastry will need to be about three sheets thick. Pile the filling into the pastry shell, then cover with four or five sheets of filo. Roll the edges of the pastry shell and lid together, folding them in over the pastry lid, then brush them well with more melted butter.

❺ Score the pastry topping into diamonds with a sharp knife, then bake the pie for 25 to 30 minutes, until the pastry is crisp and golden brown. Serve warm, cut into generous wedges.

TIP
Any filo pastry sheets left over can be wrapped in plastic wrap and put in the freezer for later use.

Butternut Squash and Cauliflower Bake

This is more filling than a cauliflower cheese, and provides the ideal "comfort food" dish.

SERVES 4

- 1 butternut squash (weighing about 2 lb 4 oz)
- 1 large onion, chopped fine
- 3 Tbsp olive oil
- 1–2 tsp sweet Spanish paprika
- 1 small cauliflower, weighing about 14 oz, cut into florets
- 2 x 14-oz cans chopped tomatoes
- 2 Tbsp chopped fresh tarragon
- 1 Tbsp caraway seeds (optional)
- 1–2 garlic cloves, sliced fine
- Salt and ground black pepper
- About 1 cup well-flavored vegetable stock
- 2 cups fresh whole wheat bread crumbs
- 1½ cups shredded Monterey Jack cheese

Preparation: 15 minutes

Cooking time: 1½ hours

❶ Preheat a 375°F oven. Cut the squash in half and remove the seeds, then peel away the skin with a sharp knife. Cut the flesh into roughly 1-inch pieces.

❷ Cook the onion in the oil for 3 to 4 minutes in a flameproof casserole, then stir in the squash and paprika. Cook for 2 to 3 minutes more, then add the cauliflower, tomatoes, tarragon, caraway seeds, if using, garlic, and seasoning. Add sufficient stock to almost cover the vegetables, then bring to a boil. Cover the casserole dish and cook in the oven for 1 hour.

❸ Mix together the bread crumbs and cheese, then scatter the topping over the vegetables. Increase the oven temperature to 400°F, then bake, uncovered, for 15 to 20 minutes more, until the topping has browned. Serve immediately, with fresh crusty bread and freshly cooked green vegetables if you like.

Mediterranean Baked Stuffed Squash

The sunshine flavors of the Mediterranean baked in a squash. This is a very satisfying dish.

SERVES 4

- 2 small squash, such as acorn or red kuri, weighing about 1 lb 10 oz each
- Salt and ground black pepper
- Olive oil

FOR THE FILLING

- 4 large scallions, chopped fine
- 1 garlic clove, crushed
- 6 halves sun-dried tomatoes in oil, sliced
- 1 small green zucchini, trimmed and diced
- 1 small yellow zucchini, trimmed and diced
- 10 large green olives, pitted and chopped
- 1 cup fresh whole wheat bread crumbs
- 2 Tbsp chopped fresh parsley
- 2–3 Tbsp oil from the tomatoes or melted butter

Preparation: 15 minutes
Cooking time: 25 minutes

❶ Preheat a 425°F oven. Cut the squash in half and scoop out the seeds, then trim the base of each piece so that the shells will sit flat. Place the shells, cut side up, in a large roasting pan. Season lightly, then drizzle with olive oil. Roast the squash for 10 minutes whilst preparing the filling.

❷ Mix all the ingredients for the filling together with plenty of seasoning. Bind together with oil or melted butter, then spoon into the part-roasted squash shells. Mound the filling in the shells, return to the oven, and continue cooking for 20 to 25 minutes, until the filling is browned and the squash are tender.

❸ Serve immediately, with freshly cooked vegetables or a mixed salad.

Roasted Pumpkin Ratatouille Cobbler

A great dish for hungry vegetarians and meat-eaters alike. The hot roasting oven used for the pumpkin is further employed to finish the dish, baking the cheese biscuit topping. Serve with freshly cooked vegetables of your choice.

SERVES 4–6

- 6 x 1-in thick slices peeled, seeded pumpkin (weighing about 1 lb 10 oz)
- Salt and ground black pepper
- Olive oil
- 1 large onion, chopped
- 2 green bell peppers, sliced
- 1 eggplant, diced
- 2 zucchini, diced
- 1–2 garlic cloves, sliced fine
- 2 cups puréed tomatoes or thick tomato juice

FOR THE TOPPING

- 1½ cups flour
- 1½ tsp baking powder
- 1 tsp mustard powder
- Pinch of salt
- ½ stick butter
- ⅔ cup shredded Monterey Jack cheese
- About ⅔ cup cold milk
- Sour cream, to serve (optional)

Preparation: 1 hour

Cooking time: 20–25 minutes

---

❶ Preheat a 425°F oven. Arrange the pumpkin slices in a small roasting pan, season, then drizzle with olive oil. Roast for 40 to 45 minutes.

❷ Cook the onion in 3 tablespoons olive oil in an ovenproof casserole dish until soft, then add the bell peppers and eggplant. Toss the vegetables in the hot oil, then cook them slowly for 3 to 4 minutes. Stir in the diced zucchini and garlic, then add the puréed tomatoes or tomato juice. Season well, then bring slowly to a boil. Cover and simmer for 20 to 25 minutes, then season to taste.

❸ Remove the pumpkin from the oven and let stand until cool. Cut the flesh away from the skin and chop into 1-inch dice. Add the pumpkin to the ratatouille and stir in any extra seasoning.

❹ Stir together flour, baking powder, mustard, and salt, then blend in the butter until the mixture resembles fine bread crumbs. Stir in the cheese, then mix to a soft but

manageable dough with the milk. Knead lightly on a floured surface, then roll into eight rough balls and drop into the top of the ratatouille.

❺ Bake for 18 to 20 minutes, until the biscuit topping is golden brown and well risen. Serve immediately, with a dollop of sour cream if using.

Curried Banana Squash

This curry is stir-fried, and simple and quick to prepare. Make it as mild or as hot as you like, according to the strength of curry powder.

SERVES 4

FOR THE CURRY PASTE

- 2 large onions, chopped
- 4 garlic cloves, chopped
- 2-in piece fresh ginger root, peeled
- 1 hot red chile, deseeded and chopped
- 1–2 Tbsp curry powder
- 1 Tbsp tomato paste
- 1 tsp salt
- 1 cup blanched almonds
- 3 Tbsp peanut oil

- 5 cups diced banana squash
- ⅓ cup crumbled creamed coconut
- 1 cup water
- Salt and ground black pepper

Preparation: 10 minutes
Cooking time: 25 minutes

❶ Blend all the ingredients for the curry paste together in a blender or food processor until smooth. Fry the almonds in oil, until golden.

❷ Remove almonds and add the squash to the pan. Cook quickly until starting to brown, then stir in the curry paste. Fry for 2 to 3 minutes, then add the creamed coconut, and stir until melted.

❸ Add the water, then bring the curry to a boil. Simmer for 15 to 20 minutes. Just before serving, add the almonds and stir to warm through. Adjust the seasoning.

Squash Stuffed Roasted Bell Peppers

Red bell peppers are much sweeter than green for baking or roasting; yellow are the next best.

SERVES 4

- 4 large red bell peppers
- 4 cups diced, prepared, firm-fleshed squash, such as crown prince, acorn, or kabocha
- 2 large garlic cloves, sliced fine
- Salt and ground black pepper
- 4 fresh tomatoes, skinned, halved, deseeded
- 1¼ cups light cream
- ½ cup freshly shredded Parmesan cheese
- Olive oil

Preparation: 15 minutes
Cooking time: 35 minutes

❶ Preheat a 425°F oven. Cut the bell peppers in half lengthwise through the stalk. Remove the core and seeds. Rinse and arrange the peppers in a suitable ovenproof dish.

❷ Pile the diced squash into the bell peppers, burying the sliced garlic in amongst the pieces. Season well, then top with the halved tomatoes.

❸ Mix the cream with the Parmesan cheese and a little more seasoning, then carefully pour the mixture into the bell peppers.

❹ Drizzle a little olive oil over, then bake at the top of the hot oven for 30 to 35 minutes, until the bell peppers are starting to blacken and the cheese is browned.

❺ Serve hot, perhaps with a few salad leaves or stir-fried zucchini.

main course vegetable dishes

Pumpkin and Navy Bean Cassoulet

A cassoulet is usually made with a variety of fatty meats such as goose, belly pork, ham, and garlic sausage. This is a far healthier version of the classic French dish, but retains the texture and filling characteristics of the dish that it is modeled on.

SERVES 6

- 1½ cups dried navy beans, soaked overnight
- 2 large onions, sliced
- 3 Tbsp olive oil
- 4 cups peeled, seeded, and diced pumpkin
- 2 garlic cloves, sliced
- 3 zucchini, diced
- Salt and ground black pepper
- 14-oz can chopped tomatoes
- 4 large sprigs thyme
- 3 bay leaves
- 3 cups well-flavored vegetable stock
- 3 cups fresh whole wheat bread crumbs

**Preparation: 1 hour
+ overnight soaking
Cooking time: 1½ hours**

---

❶ Drain the beans and rinse thoroughly in fresh, cold water. Bring to a boil in a large pan of fresh water, then cover, and simmer for 1 hour. Meanwhile, prepare the remaining ingredients.

❷ Preheat a 325°F oven. Cook the onions in the oil in a large flameproof casserole for 5 to 6 minutes, until soft but not browned. Add the prepared pumpkin and cook for 4 to 5 minutes more, then stir in the garlic and zucchini. Season well, then pour the chopped tomatoes over the vegetables.

❸ Drain the beans and place them in a thick layer over the vegetables, tucking the thyme and bay leaves into them. Add salt and pepper, and sufficient stock to come to just below the level of the beans. Cover the casserole and cook in the oven for 1 hour.

❹ Remove the lid of the casserole and take out the sprigs of thyme and the bay leaves. Make a thick layer of the bread crumbs over the beans. Increase the oven temperature to 400°F and return the cassoulet to the oven for 20 minutes more, until the topping is browned and crisp. Serve with just a green salad.

Baked Stuffed Patty Pan Squash

Big patty pan squashes make excellent stuffed vegetables. They have a soft skin and do not require peeling and I sometimes think the flesh has a slight hint of coconut about it. I trim off the stalk of the squash, then turn it upside-down to cut a round out of the base to scoop out the seeds. I also cook and serve the squash upside-down, as I think it looks better that way!

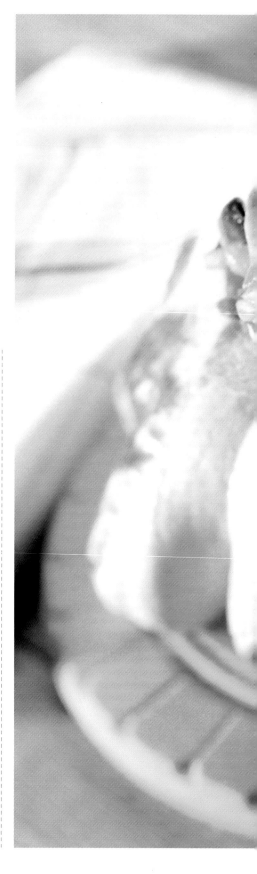

SERVES 4

- 1 patty pan squash (weighing about 2 lb 4 oz)
- Salt and ground black pepper
- 3 Tbsp extra virgin olive oil
- 1 large onion, chopped fine
- 2 celery stalks, chopped
- 1 garlic clove
- 6 oz mushrooms, sliced
- ½ tsp ground mace
- 14-oz can chopped tomatoes
- 3 Tbsp chopped fresh parsley

Preparation: 30 minutes
Cooking time: 25 minutes

❶ Preheat a 400°F oven. Cut a circle from the base of the squash and scoop out the seeds. Season the cavity and trickle 1 tablespoon of oil around it. Bake the squash in a roasting pan for 20 minutes while preparing the filling.

❷ Cook the onion and celery in the remaining oil, in a large frying pan, for 4 to 5 minutes over low heat, until softened but not browned. Stir in the garlic and mushrooms, with the mace, and cook for 2 to 3 minutes more, until the mushrooms are soft and the juices run. Add the chopped tomatoes, with a little salt and pepper, then simmer for 10 minutes, until reduced and slightly thickened. Add extra salt and pepper to taste, then stir in the parsley.

❸ Spoon the tomato and mushroom filling into the part-baked squash, then bake for 20 to 25 minutes more, until the squash is tender. Serve cut into quarters, perhaps with a lentil salad and a green leaf salad.

main course vegetable dishes

102

Blue Cheese and Pecan Risotto with Squash

A brilliant risotto, and so unusual! I prefer to use a piquant blue cheese such as English Stilton to give a tangy, sharp zing. However, a sweeter cheese, such as dolcelatte, will give a more subtle flavoring. The pecans are sweet and almost mystical in the slightly sticky rice.

SERVES 4

- Good pinch saffron threads
- 4½ cups well-flavored vegetable stock
- 2 Tbsp olive oil
- 1 tsp butter
- 1 onion, chopped fine
- 2 cups peeled, seeded, and diced squash, such as crown prince, acorn, or golden Hubbard
- 2 garlic cloves, crushed
- 1½ cups arborio rice
- 12 sage leaves, sliced
- 1 cup crumbled blue-veined cheese
- 1 cup pecans, chopped
- Salt and ground black pepper
- Dressed arugula leaves, to garnish

Preparation: 15 minutes
Cooking time: 30–40 minutes

❶ Soak the saffron in the almost boiling stock until required—keep the stock as warm as possible. Heat the oil and butter together in a large frying pan, then add the onion, and cook over low heat until softened.

❷ Add the squash and cook quite quickly, until almost starting to brown. Stir in the garlic and the rice, and toss to coat in oil.

❸ Add one third of the stock, then bring the rice to a boil, and cook, stirring frequently, until almost all the stock has been absorbed. Add half the remaining stock and repeat the cooking process, then add the sage leaves followed by the remaining stock. Continue cooking until most of the stock has been absorbed, then stir in the crumbled cheese and the pecans.

❹ Continue cooking until the cheese has just melted, then remove the pan from the heat, and season the mixture well. Serve garnished.

TIP
Substitute walnuts for the pecans, if you wish, but only use ½ cup as their dominant flavor can easily overpower the dish.

Squash and Okra Curry

The secret with okra is to cook it for quite a long time, until the texture is somewhat sticky. Instead of banana squash, you could use acorn or golden Hubbard.

SERVES 3–4

FOR THE CURRY PASTE

- 1 large onion, chopped
- 2–3 garlic cloves, chopped
- 1 Tbsp curry powder
- 2 green chiles, deseeded and chopped
- 2 Tbsp lime or prawn relish
- 1 Tbsp Demerara sugar
- 1 tsp salt
- 1 Tbsp tomato paste

- 4 cups peeled, seeded, and diced banana squash
- 3 Tbsp peanut oil, plus extra
- 1 lb okra, trimmed and cut into ½-in slices
- 1 cup water or vegetable stock
- 14-oz can chickpeas, drained
- 2–3 Tbsp chopped fresh cilantro
- Plain yogurt and rice, or Indian flat breads, to serve

Preparation: 10 minutes

Cooking time: 1 hour

❶ Blend all the ingredients for the curry paste together in a blender or food processor. Add a little oil or water to make a smooth paste.

❷ Cook the squash in the oil in a large pan for 4 to 5 minutes, then add the okra. Sauté the vegetables together for 2 to 3 minutes.

❸ Scrape the curry paste into the pan, cook over low heat for 4 to 5 minutes, then add the water or stock. Bring to a boil, then simmer the curry for 40 minutes, until the squash and the okra are tender.

❹ Stir in the drained chickpeas and cook for 5 minutes more. Season a little more if necessary, then add the chopped cilantro, and serve.

Savory Country Pumpkin Pie

A simple vegetable pie, but one that is full of texture and flavor. Use as wide a selection of vegetables as you can; you could even use two or three varieties of squash which should make up about one third of the total. The capers add a touch of the exotic, and you could use a blue cheese, goat cheese, or Parmesan instead of Monterey Jack, if you prefer.

SERVES 4–5

• 2 lb 4 oz potatoes

• 2 lb 4 oz mixed vegetables, cut into 1-in chunks, such as pumpkin, parsnips, carrots, onions, leeks, and zucchini

• 3 Tbsp capers

• Salt and ground black pepper

• 4 cups milk

• ½ stick butter

• 4 Tbsp flour

• 1¼ cups shredded Monterey Jack cheese

Preparation: 35 minutes

Cooking time: 50 minutes

---

❶ Preheat a 375°F oven and butter a large gratin dish. Bring the potatoes to a boil in a large pan of salted water, then simmer for 5 minutes. Drain and leave to cool.

❷ Bring another large pan of water to a boil, then add all the prepared vegetables. Return to a boil, then simmer for 10 minutes. Drain thoroughly in a colander, turn into the prepared dish, and add the capers with some salt and pepper.

❸ Slice the potatoes and arrange them over the vegetables. Combine the milk, butter, and flour in a pan and bring slowly to a boil, stirring all the time. Continue to cook the sauce for 1 minute, until thickened, then add the cheese and seasoning to taste. Pour the sauce over the potatoes and spread it evenly. Place the gratin dish on a baking sheet if it is very full.

❹ Bake the pie for 45 to 50 minutes, until the topping is well browned. Serve in generous portions, with freshly cooked green vegetables, such as broccoli, fava beans, or French beans.

Kabocha, Fennel, and Orange Casserole

I have always liked the combination of fennel and orange. Add some kabocha squash and you have a satisfying and tasty casserole to serve with brown rice.

SERVES 4

- 1 lb 2 oz peeled, seeded kabocha squash, cut into 1-in pieces
- 4 Tbsp extra virgin olive oil
- 1 large onion, chopped
- 4 celery stalks, chopped
- 1 large fennel bulb, trimmed and sliced fine
- ½ cup lentils
- 14-oz can chopped tomatoes
- 1 cup well-flavored vegetable stock
- Salt and ground black pepper
- 3 bay leaves
- 1 Tbsp chopped fresh sage
- Grated rind and chopped flesh of 2 oranges
- 1 cup pecans
- Cooked brown rice, to serve

Preparation: 15 minutes

Cooking time: 1 hour

❶ Cook the squash in the oil in a large saucepan until just starting to brown and soften. This will take about 4 to 5 minutes over medium-high heat. Stir in the onion, celery, and fennel, reduce the heat, and cook gently for 3 to 4 minutes, until soft.

❷ Add the lentils, tomatoes, and stock with some seasoning, the bay leaves, and sage. Bring to a boil, then simmer very gently for 30 to 40 minutes, until the squash is tender.

❸ Stir in the chopped orange and the nuts, and cook for 1 to 2 minutes more, just to heat through. Remove the bay leaves and adjust the seasoning if necessary. Serve the casserole on a bed of brown rice, garnished with the orange rind and any fronds from the fennel bulb.

TIP

The ideal garnish for this dish are the feathery fronds from the top of the fennel bulb.

main course vegetable dishes

Squash and Apricot Bulgur Risotto

The coarse grains of bulgur wheat make an excellent alternative to rice for this risotto, which has a very exciting combination of fruity flavors and vegetables.

SERVES 4

- 1 large onion, sliced
- 1 leek, trimmed and sliced
- 2 Tbsp olive oil
- 3 cups diced, prepared squash, such as crown prince
- 1 tsp ground cumin
- 1 tsp ground ginger
- 1–2 plump garlic cloves, sliced fine
- 4 celery stalks, sliced
- 1 red bell pepper, sliced
- 1½ cups bulgur wheat
- ½ cup ready-to-eat dried apricots, chopped
- 2 cups chopped tomatoes
- 3 cups water or stock
- Salt and ground black pepper
- 1 cup snow peas, topped and tailed
- 6 halves sun-dried tomatoes, shredded

Preparation: 15 minutes
Cooking time: 30 minutes

❶ Cook the onion and leek in the oil until softened but not browned, then add the squash and spices, and cook for 2 to 3 minutes more. Add the garlic, celery, and bell pepper, then cook briefly before stirring in the bulgur wheat and apricots.

❷ Add the tomatoes, stock, and seasoning, then simmer for 12 to 15 minutes, stirring occasionally.

❸ Add the snow peas and sun-dried tomatoes, and cook for 4 to 5 minutes more. Serve immediately, with a tossed green salad.

Spiced Pumpkin Soufflé

Soufflés are actually very easy to make. The only difficulty is that they don't stay light and fluffy for very long, so rounding up your guests is actually more important than your technique!

SERVES 3

- ¼ stick butter
- 1 Tbsp fine whole wheat flour
- 1 tsp ground cumin
- 1 tsp ground ginger
- ⅔ cup milk
- 1 cup thick pumpkin purée
- 1 tsp Dijon mustard
- 3 large eggs, separated
- Salt and ground black pepper

Preparation: 15 minutes
Cooking time: 40 minutes

❶ Preheat a 350°F oven. Lightly butter a 6 to 7-inch soufflé dish.

❷ Heat the butter in a small pan, then stir in the flour with the spices, and cook for 1 minute, stirring all the time. Off the heat, gradually beat in the milk, then bring slowly to a boil, stirring all the time. Cook for 1 minute, then stir in the pumpkin purée, mustard, and egg yolks.

❸ Whisk the egg whites until stiff then fold them into the pumpkin mixture. Scrape the soufflé into the prepared dish, bake for 30 to 40 minutes, until set, then serve.

Pumpkin Pancake Galette

Pumpkin, Rum, and Raisin Ice Cream

Green Fruit Salad

Melon Sherbet

Date and Pumpkin Cake

Pumpkin and Prune Tart

Pumpkin and Fig Bread

Melon and Orange Compote with Almond Cake

Kabocha Bread

Squash and Apple Almond Strudel

Zucchini Passion Cake

Pumpkin and Lemon Roulade

Pumpkin and Pecan Cornmeal Muffins

Pumpkin and Raisin Pie

Squash and Celery Cheese Bread

Pumpkin Pancake Galette

These flavorful pancakes are a little starchy, so they are easiest to cook in a nonstick pan.

SERVES 4

- 8 oz cooked firm-fleshed pumpkin
- ¾ cup flour
- 2 large eggs
- 1¼ cups milk
- 1 Tbsp vegetable oil
- Pinch of salt
- Freshly grated ½ nutmeg
- Vegetable oil, for frying

TO SERVE

- Stewed apple made from 1 lb 2 oz tart cooking apples and sugar to taste
- Maple syrup

Preparation: 10 minutes

Cooking time: 15 minutes

❶ Peel and chop the cooked pumpkin, then place it in a blender or food processor with all the other batter ingredients, and blend until smooth and thick.

❷ Heat a little oil in a nonstick omelet pan, then add about one quarter of the batter. Cook the pancake until set and browned on the underside, then flip it over, and cook briefly on the second side until browned. Continue until all the batter has been used.

❸ On a serving platter, layer the pancakes with the stewed apple and a generous drizzle of maple syrup. Reheat either in a microwave or a medium oven, then top with extra maple syrup before serving.

TIP

This pancake mixture also makes very good griddle cakes.

Pumpkin, Rum, and Raisin Ice Cream

If you don't like rum and raisin ice cream, don't be put off, this is delicious! It is also a very good way of using up half a can of pumpkin purée!

SERVES 6–8

- 4 large egg yolks
- 1 tsp freshly grated nutmeg
- ½ cup light brown sugar
- 1¼ cups full-fat milk
- About ¼ cup dark rum
- 1 cup canned pumpkin purée
- 1¼ cups light cream
- ½ cup seedless raisins

Preparation: 2½ hours

Freezing time: 4–5 hours

❶ Whisk together the egg yolks, nutmeg, and sugar until thick. Heat the milk until almost boiling, then pour it on to the egg mixture, whisking all the time. Rinse the pan, then return the custard, and cook gently until thickened just enough to coat the back of a wooden spoon. Pour the custard into a clean bowl and let cool completely. When cooled, chill for 1 hour.

❷ Stir the rum and pumpkin purée into the custard, then add the cream. Freeze the ice cream in a plastic box in the freezer for 4 to 5 hours, whisking or beating two or three times during freezing. Add the raisins just before the ice cream is ready. Harden the ice cream in a

suitable covered plastic container for at least 30 minutes before serving—this is necessary because of the amount of rum in the mixture.

Alternatively, you can turn into an ice-cream machine and freeze-churn until thick.

Green Fruit Salad

Refreshing and ultra-simple, all this dessert requires is a little time to prepare the fruits with care. The grapes are better skinned, if you have the inclination.

SERVES 6

- 1 small ripe Galia melon, scooped into balls
- 1 small ripe honeydew melon, scooped into balls
- 4 ripe kiwi fruits, peeled and chopped
- Green grapes – as many as you like—deseeded and halved
- 1–2 Tbsp chopped fresh mint
- 2–3 Tbsp melon liqueur (optional)
- Superfine sugar (optional)

Preparation: 40 minutes
Chilling time: 30 minutes

❶ Combine all the fruits in a large decorative serving bowl, adding any juices from the melons.

❷ Stir in the mint, and the liqueur if using. Add just a little sugar if the melons are underripe.

❸ Chill the fruits for no more than 30 minutes before serving.

TIP

If you can, use apple mint or pineapple mint in this salad. Their fruity flavors are ideal.

Melon Sherbet

I have used a Galia melon to make this light, refreshing ice but it is just as successful made with watermelon.

SERVES 6

- 1½ cups full-fat milk
- ½ cup superfine sugar
- 2 cups Galia melon purée
- 1 Tbsp lemon juice
- 1 Tbsp chopped fresh mint

Preparation: 1 hour
Freezing time: 4–5 hours

❶ Heat the milk and sugar together gently until the sugar has dissolved, then bring to a boil. Simmer the syrup for 15 minutes, then pour it into a clean bowl, and let cool completely.

❷ Blend the melon purée with the sweetened milk, lemon juice, and mint. Turn the mixture into a suitable plastic tub and place in the freezer for 4 to 5 hours. Remember to stir the sherbet thoroughly twice during this time. Alternatively, turn the mixture into an ice-cream machine and freeze-churn until thick and quite firm. Serve immediately or freeze until required.

TIP

Make certain that the melon is really ripe to get the best possible flavor—it should be very fragrant through the skin, but not soft in the flesh.

Green Fruit Salad

Date and Pumpkin Cake

Adding pumpkin purée to a cake keeps it moist and succulent. This cake is just as good as a dessert, with morning coffee, or afternoon tea. I sometimes serve it with a spoonful of unsweetened yogurt.

SERVES 8

- ⅔ cup flour, sifted
- 1 tsp baking powder
- 1 tsp baking soda
- 2 tsp pumpkin pie spice
- ½ cup chopped dates
- ½ cup chopped pecans
- 2 Tbsp flour
- ½ stick butter
- 1 cup light brown sugar
- 1 cup pumpkin purée, fresh or canned
- 2 large eggs, beaten
- Whipped cream and grated chocolate, to decorate

Preparation: 15 minutes

Cooking time: 30 minutes

❶ Preheat a 350°F oven. Line a 9-inch round cake pan with baking parchment.

❷ Sift together the flour, raising agents, and pumpkin pie spice. Mix the dates with the pecans and toss them in the 2 tablespoons flour.

❸ Melt the butter over low heat, add the sugar, and stir into a thick paste. Stir in the pumpkin, then gradually add the beaten eggs. Add the dry ingredients, then beat in the floured dates and nuts. Mix thoroughly to a thick batter, then scoop into the prepared pan.

❹ Bake in the oven for about 30 minutes, or until a skewer inserted into the center of the cake comes out clean. Let cool slightly, then remove from the pan, and let cool completely on a wire rack.

❺ Serve decorated with whipped cream and grated chocolate.

desserts and baking

114

Pumpkin and Prune Tart

A light prune tart with a melt-in-the-mouth egg custard is one of my favorite desserts. I have now created a variation on a family recipe, and added pumpkin to the custard.

SERVES 6–8

FOR THE PASTRY
- ½ stick butter
- 1¼ cups flour
- 1 tsp superfine sugar
- Cold water, to mix

FOR THE FILLING
- 1 cup thick pumpkin purée, fresh or canned
- 2 large eggs, beaten
- Freshly grated ¼ nutmeg
- 3 Tbsp light brown sugar
- 1 cup milk
- ½ cup chopped, pitted, ready-to-eat prunes
- ⅓ cup toasted hazelnuts, chopped

Preparation: 1 hour
Cooking time: 45 minutes

❶ Prepare the pastry by blending the butter into the flour and sugar until the mixture resembles fine bread crumbs, then add sufficient cold water to bind to a stiff dough. Knead gently on a lightly floured surface, then roll out, and use to line a deep, preferably loose-based 8-inch pie pan. Chill for 30 minutes.

❷ Preheat a 400°F oven. Spread half the pumpkin purée over the base of the pastry shell, then beat the remainder with the eggs, nutmeg, and brown sugar. Gradually beat in the milk. Scatter the chopped prunes and nuts over the pastry, then pour the pumpkin custard into the pastry shell.

❸ Grate a little more nutmeg over the filling, then bake for 15 minutes. Lower the temperature to 375°F and bake for 25 to 30 minutes more, until the pastry is browned and the filling has set.

❹ Allow the tart to cool slightly, then carefully remove it from the pan. Serve warm or cold.

Pumpkin and Fig Bread

A moist fruit loaf to serve just buttered, or with jelly. The figs contribute a definite flavor to the loaf, so I tend to serve it on its own, with a reviving cup of tea. I have used fast-acting dried yeast for this loaf, so it only requires one rising period.

MAKES 1 LARGE LOAF

- 4¼ cups strong white bread flour
- 2 Tbsp superfine sugar
- 1 tsp salt
- 1 sachet dried yeast
- ¾ cup ready-to-eat dried figs, chopped
- 1 cup thick pumpkin purée, fresh or canned
- 1 cup warm water, plus extra
- Beaten egg, to glaze (optional)

Preparation: 1½ hours
Cooking time: 40 minutes
---

❶ Mix the flour, sugar, and salt together in a large bowl, then stir in the dried yeast and chopped figs. Make a well in the center, add the pumpkin purée, and most of the water. Mix to a soft, manageable dough, adding extra water as necessary. Turn out onto a lightly floured surface and knead thoroughly, until the dough is smooth and elastic, 5 to 10 minutes.

❷ Shape the dough and place either on a baking sheet or in a large loaf pan. I like to make this bread in a pan—I always think the regular shape is so much easier to slice. Leave to rise for about 1 hour, covered with a damp dish towel or plastic wrap.

❸ Preheat a 425°F oven toward the end of the rising period. Brush the loaf with a little beaten egg, if you wish—this will give a really high glaze—or sprinkle it with a little flour. Bake for 35 to 40 minutes, until the bread is well browned and the base sounds hollow when tapped. Let cool on a wire rack before slicing.

Melon and Orange Compote with Almond Cake

This delightful dessert is redolent of the flavors of Spain—ripe, juicy melons and oranges, almonds, and fragrant, melon-scented olive oil.

SERVES 6–8

FOR THE ORANGE AND ALMOND CAKE

- 3 large eggs, separated
- ⅔ cup superfine sugar
- Grated rind and juice of 1 large orange
- ¼ cup blanched almonds, toasted and chopped fine
- ⅔ cup ground almonds
- ½ cup light brown sugar
- Almond extract
- Flaked almonds, to decorate
  1 ripe Galia melon, scooped into balls
- Pared rind of 2 large oranges
- 2–3 Tbsp extra virgin Spanish olive oil

Preparation: 40 minutes
Cooking time: 40 minutes

❶ Preheat a 350°F oven. Line a loose-based, deep, 8-inch cake pan with baking parchment.

❷ For the cake, whisk the egg yolks with the sugar and orange rind until thick, then whisk in the chopped and ground almonds—the mixture will become very thick. In a separate bowl, whisk the egg whites until stiff, then fold them quickly and lightly into the mixture. Scrape and pour the cake into the cake pan,

lightly level the top, then bake for about 40 minutes.

❸ Line a cooling rack with baking parchment, then carefully turn the cake out onto the rack. Take great care as the cake is very delicate. Leave to cool.

❹ Squeeze the juice from the orange and make up to 1¼ cups with fresh orange juice. Heat with the brown sugar and bring slowly to a boil, stirring to dissolve the sugar, then boil for 3 to 4 minutes until slightly

syrupy. Then add a few drops of almond extract.

❺ Invert the cake onto a serving plate and prick it all over with a fine skewer. Spoon the syrup through the cake, allowing it to soak in well, then leave for at least 1 hour. Scatter with the flaked almonds.

❻ For the compote, combine the melon balls and pared orange rinds, then add the olive oil. Spoon the fruit around the almond cake. Serve cut into wedges with plenty of fruit.

Kabocha Bread

Kabochas are a very popular New Zealand squash but this bread could also be made with buttercup.

MAKES 2 LARGE LOAVES

- 1 kabocha squash (weighing about 2 lb 4 oz)
- Salt and ground black pepper
- Olive oil, for drizzling
- 1 oz fresh yeast
- 1¼ cups lukewarm water
- 6 cups strong white bread flour
- 1 Tbsp salt
- 1 Tbsp Dijon mustard
- 3 Tbsp olive oil

Preparation: 2 hours
Cooking time: 40 minutes

---

❶ Preheat a 425°F oven. Cut the squash into six and remove the seeds, then place in a small roasting pan, and season lightly. Drizzle with a little olive oil and roast for 45 minutes. Let cool completely. Scoop the flesh from the skin, then blend until smooth in a blender or food processor.

❷ Crumble the yeast into the warm water, leave for 2 to 3 minutes, then stir to make sure it has dissolved completely. Mix the flour with the salt in a large bowl, and mix the mustard with the puréed squash. Make a well in the middle of the flour and add the olive oil, kabocha

purée, and the yeast liquid. Mix to a smooth manageable dough, adding more flour or water as necessary.

❸ Knead the dough until smooth and elastic, then flour the bowl, and return the dough. Cover and leave in a warm place for about 1 hour.

❹ Turn out onto a lightly floured work surface and knead. Divide in two, then shape each piece into a long fat sausage. Place on a lightly greased and floured baking sheet, cover with a damp cloth, and leave to rise again for 30 to 40 minutes.

❺ Preheat a 425°F oven. Slash the loaves diagonally a number of times, then bake for 35 to 40 minutes, until a dark golden color. The base of the loaves will sound hollow when tapped if they are completely cooked. Leave to cool on a wire rack for at least 15 minutes before eating.

TIP

If you wish, use fast-rising dried yeast. Simply add one sachet to the flour, then shape the dough and allow one rising only.

desserts and baking

Squash and Apple Almond Strudel

I am constantly amazed at how much flavor squash will give to a dessert. An apple strudel becomes something quite different with the addition of squash—a filling but not too sweet dessert to serve after a light main course.

SERVES 6

- ¼ stick butter
- 2 cups peeled, seeded, and diced kabocha squash
- 1 tsp ground ginger
- Crushed seeds from 5 green cardamom pods
- 2 Tbsp light brown sugar
- 1 cup cream cheese
- 1 sharp green eating apple, cored and cut into ¼-in dice
- Grated rind and juice of 1 lemon
- ⅓ cup toasted almonds, chopped
- 8–10 sheets filo pastry
- ¼ stick butter, melted
- Sifted confectioners' sugar, for dredging

Preparation: 20 minutes

Cooking time: 25 minutes

❶ Preheat a 400°F oven. Melt the butter in a small pan, add the squash, ginger, and cardamom seeds, and cook gently for 4 to 5 minutes, until the squash is just soft, stirring occasionally. Then add the sugar.

❷ Beat the cream cheese until soft, then add the squash with the apple, lemon rind and juice, and the almonds. Mix well, then set aside.

❸ Lightly butter a baking sheet, then arrange the filo pastry sheets on it, overlapping them and stacking into a rectangle about 12 x 14 inches, approximately four pastry sheets thick. Brush each pastry sheet with melted butter to keep it moist. Pile the filling in a long line in the middle of the pastry, then fold over the two sides and the bottom of the sheet. Roll the strudel up as for a spring roll, tucking the join under the strudel on the baking sheet.

❹ Brush with any remaining melted butter, then bake for 25 minutes, until the pastry is a rich golden brown. Let cool slightly, then transfer to a serving plate, and dredge lightly with confectioners' sugar. Serve warm direct from the oven, or wait until cooled.

Zucchini Passion Cake

Passion cake is usually made with carrots and often looks very healthy and wholesome! Despite this, it is wickedly delicious. However, for a more festive-looking cake, I add shredded zucchini for extra color—use some green and some yellow if possible.

SERVES 10–12

- 2 cups all-purpose flour
- 2 tsp baking powder
- 1 tsp baking soda
- 1 tsp salt
- 1 cup superfine sugar
- ⅓ cup pine nuts
- ⅓ cup raisins
- 2 ripe bananas, mashed
- 3 large eggs, beaten
- 2 cups shredded mixed carrots and zucchini
- ⅔ cup peanut or vegetable oil

FOR THE FROSTING

- ⅔ cup cream cheese
- 1 stick butter, softened
- ½ tsp vanilla extract
- 2 cups sifted confectioners' sugar
- Shredded mixed carrot and zucchini, to decorate (optional)

**Preparation: 15 minutes +
45 minutes for frosting
Cooking time: 1 hour**

❶ Preheat a 350°F oven. Line a deep 9-inch cake pan with baking parchment—springform is best.

❷ Sift the flour, baking powder, baking soda, and salt into a large mixing bowl, then add the sugar, pine nuts, and golden raisins. Mix well, then add the mashed bananas and beaten eggs. Stir in the shredded vegetables and finally the oil, then beat the cake thoroughly for 1 minute, to a thick, slightly lumpy batter.

❸ Scrape the batter into the prepared pan then bake for 1 hour, or until a skewer inserted into the center of the cake comes out clean. Leave for a few minutes, then carefully remove the cake from the pan and let cool completely.

❹ To make the frosting, beat the cream cheese and butter together with the vanilla until smooth, then gradually beat in the sugar. Let stand in a cool place for about 30 minutes, to harden slightly, then spread over the cake. A little shredded mixed carrot and zucchini makes a perfect decoration, either in tiny mounds around the edge of the cake, or in the center.

Pumpkin and Lemon Roulade

Surprisingly light and tangy, this roulade makes a very pleasant change from the more traditional pumpkin pie. An excellent dessert for the early days of fall when a little culinary comfort is required, but nothing too heavy. I find that the best way of folding the flour into the whisked egg mixture quickly and lightly is with a wire whisk, not a metal spoon.

SERVES 8

- 3 large eggs
- 1/3 cup superfine sugar
- 1/2 cup flour, sifted twice
- Grated rind and juice of 1 large lemon
- 2/3 cup heavy cream
- 3 Tbsp confectioners' sugar, sifted
- 1 cup thick pumpkin purée, fresh or canned
- 1/3 cup seedless raisins
- Sugar, for dredging

Preparation: 15 minutes
Cooking time: 10 minutes

---

❶ Preheat a 425°F oven. Line a 13 x 9-inch jelly roll pan with baking parchment.

❷ Whisk the eggs and sugar together until pale and very thick— you should be able to leave a figure-of-eight from the beaters trail clearly visible in the mixture. Fold the flour and lemon rind quickly into the mixture, then scrape it into the pan, and gently level the surface, shaking it into the corners.

❸ Bake for 8 to 10 minutes, until spongy in texture and golden brown. Turn the cake onto a wire rack covered with baking parchment and sprinkled with superfine sugar. Trim away the crusts of the sponge and make a shallow cut a little way in from one of the short sides, then place another piece of parchment over the sponge. Roll it up and leave, rolled up with the paper, until cold.

❹ Whip the cream until almost stiff, then add the sugar and pumpkin. Beat well, then fold in the raisins. Unwrap the roulade and remove the inner paper. Spread the cream over the sponge, then reroll it using the sugared paper to help. Transfer to a plate.

❺ Pierce the cake right through in lots of places with a thin skewer. Drizzle the lemon juice over the roulade. Dredge with more superfine sugar, then leave for about 20 minutes before serving, to allow the lemon to flavor the sponge.

Pumpkin and Pecan Cornmeal Muffins

The reason that I often add cornmeal to a muffin mix is that it makes them a little more grainy and interesting in texture. Fine polenta also works well.

MAKES 12

- 1 Tbsp butter
- 1 cup fine whole wheat flour
- ½ cup cornmeal or fine polenta
- 1 tsp ground ginger
- 1 tsp baking powder
- ½ tsp baking soda
- ½ cup pecans, chopped
- 1 large egg, beaten
- ¾ cup thick pumpkin purée, fresh or canned
- ¾ cup buttermilk
- Brown sugar crystals, to decorate

Preparation: 20 minutes
Cooking time: 30 minutes

❶ Preheat a 350°F oven. Carefully line 12 deep muffin pans with muffin paper cases.

❷ Melt the butter in a small saucepan, then let cool. Mix together all the dry ingredients in a bowl, then add the nuts. Beat the egg with the pumpkin purée and the buttermilk, then add the melted butter. Tip the paste into the flour mixture, then mix the muffin batter together quickly, using either a metal spoon or a spatula.

❸ Divide the mixture among the paper cases and bake for 25 to 30 minutes, until set and browned. The muffins are cooked when a fine skewer that has been inserted into them comes out clean.

❹ Scatter a few sugar crystals over each hot cake, pressing them lightly into the crumb, then let cool slightly before eating warm.

desserts and baking

124

Pumpkin and Raisin Pie

I have always loved this recipe because the pumpkin stays in slices, mixed with buttery, nutmeg-coated raisins. It makes a very unusual pie, a welcome change from traditional, custard-based recipes.

SERVES 6–8

- 1 lb 9 oz peeled, seeded pumpkin
- ½ cup light brown sugar
- 1 tsp butter
- ½ cup raisins
- Freshly grated nutmeg, to taste

FOR THE PASTRY

- ¾ stick butter
- 2¼ cups fine whole wheat flour
- Pinch of salt
- Warm water, to mix

Preparation: 40 minutes

Cooking time: 40 minutes

❶ Preheat a 400°F oven. Lightly butter a deep 10-inch pie pan.

❷ Cut the pumpkin into 1-inch pieces, then slice them thinly. Layer the pumpkin with the sugar in a saucepan and dot with slivers of butter. Cover the pan, then cook over low heat for 10 to 12 minutes. Shake the pan occasionally to stop the pumpkin from burning.

❸ Blend the butter into the flour and salt until the mixture resembles fine bread crumbs, then mix to a firm but manageable dough with warm water. Knead lightly on a floured surface, then divide the dough into two. Roll out one half and use to line the pie pan.

❹ Stir the raisins into the pumpkin with a generous amount of freshly grated nutmeg. Pile the filling into the pastry shell, scooping it from the pan with a slotted spoon. Reserve the juices to serve with the pie. Roll out the remaining pastry and use to cover the pie, damping the edges to seal together. Crimp the edges.

❺ Bake for 35 to 40 minutes, until well browned. Serve cut into slices with custard or cream, and the pumpkin juices spooned over.

TIP

This pie is made with a whole wheat pastry. It is much easier to bind a whole wheat dough with warm water, rather than cold.

desserts and baking

125

Squash and Celery Cheese Bread

A pumpkin picnic loaf that is really a meal in itself, but is also delicious with a soft creamy cheese—a goat cheese would be my first choice. I love the combination of the celery and pumpkin—it works really well.

MAKES 1 LOAF

- 4 celery stalks
- 1 garlic clove, quartered
- ⅔ cup water
- 2 cups whole wheat bread flour
- 2 cups strong white flour
- ½ tsp salt
- ½ oz fresh yeast
- 1 cup diced cold roast squash (use a firm-fleshed variety, such as crown prince or acorn)
- ¾ cup shredded Monterey Jack cheese

Preparation: 2½ hours
Cooking time: 40 minutes

---

❶ Reserve any leaves from the celery, then chop the stalks finely. Place in a small pan with the garlic and water, and bring to a boil. Cover the pan and simmer for 10 minutes.

Drain and reserve the water, making it up to 1½ cups with cold water. Set the celery aside.

❷ Sift the flours together with the salt into a bowl. Crumble the yeast into the luke warm celery-flavored water, leave for 2 to 3 minutes, then stir to make sure the yeast has dissolved. Add the liquid to the flours, then mix to a manageable dough. Knead thoroughly for about 10 minutes, until the dough is smooth, then return to the bowl, and cover with a damp cloth or plastic wrap. Leave in a warm place for about 1 hour, until doubled in size.

❸ Meanwhile, mix the squash and celery with the shredded cheese and season generously.

❹ Scrape the dough out of the bowl, knead lightly, then divide into two. Roll out each piece into a 9-inch circle, then place one round on a lightly greased or floured baking sheet. Pile the squash filling onto the bread, then damp the rim of the dough and cover with the remaining bread. Pinch the edges of the dough together to seal, then cover, and leave in a warm place for 30 to 40 minutes, until risen.

❺ Preheat a 425°F oven. Scatter a little white flour over the loaf, then bake for 40 minutes. Let cool for at least 15 minutes on a wire rack before cutting into rough wedges to serve.

Index

Index / Acknowledgments

Acknowledgments

This book is dedicated to Mr and Mrs
Upton of Slindon, West Sussex, England,
Pioneering Pumpkin Growers
Extraordinaire, who have been so
generous to me with their time, their
knowledge, and above all, their
enthusiasm. The publishers would like to
thank Philip Wilkins and Jon Bouchier for
photography.

Picture Credits

p.6, Life File, pp.7, 8, 11, 12, 13, 49, 66,
74, 76, 120, 128, Japics Photographic.